more praise for *about you*

"Dick Staub offers a cup of cold, clear water for all of those who thirst for something significant beyond the oft-superficial and bankrupt materialism of the prevailing culture."

—*Jeff Johnson, singer and songwriter,*
Windham Hill / Ark Music

"*About You* is a profound, capacious research into what we humans might both be and become as we find, focus and follow the intentionality of The Great Artist."

—*Nigel Goodwin, United Kingdom based actor*
and international arts advocate

"Dick Staub is a thoughtful, creative and insightful thinker, who journeys into the deep questions of life. *About You* is a treasure map, where Dick serves as both sage and guide, gently leading us to a broader understanding of our own humanity, its source and the fullness therein. A must read for fellow sojourners on the road to becoming fully human."

—*John Priddy, CEO, Priddy Brothers*

about
you

Fully Human,
Fully Alive

Dick Staub

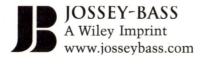

JOSSEY-BASS
A Wiley Imprint
www.josseybass.com

Published by Jossey-Bass
A Wiley Imprint
989 Market Street, San Francisco, CA 94103-1741—www.josseybass.com

All scripture quotations, unless otherwise indicated, are taken from the Holy Bible, New International Version®, NIV®. Copyright ©1973, 1978, 1984 by Biblica, Inc.™ Used by permission of Zondervan. All rights reserved worldwide. www.zondervan.com

Library of Congress Cataloging-in-Publication Data
Staub, Dick, date.
  About you : fully human, fully alive / Dick Staub.
     p. cm.
     ISBN 978-0-470-48164-6 (hardback); 978-0-470-90890-7 (ebk);
     978-0-470-90891-4 (ebk); 978-047-0-90893-8 (ebk)
 1.   Theological anthropology—Christianity. 2.   Self-actualization
 (Psychology)—Religious aspects—Christianity.   I. Title.
     BT701.3.S73 2010
     233—dc22
                                           2010013822

Printed in the United States of America
FIRST EDITION
HB Printing   10 9 8 7 6 5 4 3 2 1

contents

First and foremost to my wife, Kathy, and also to my children, Joshua, Jessica, Heidi, and Molly. Each in their own way has patiently witnessed and endured my faltering, stumbling, and often pathetic crawl toward understanding and embodying what it means to become fully alive and fully human. They are my teachers and friends for the journey and though I am a slow learner, they have consistently offered their kindness, forgiveness, and grace. Our family has learned that when it is all said and done, it all comes down to love, just as Jesus said.

preface: our shared story

recently saw a T-shirt that read: "Born for greatness but biding my time." We laugh but instantly know what it means: most of us aren't living up to our fullest potential. Would you like to make sense of your life? Do you want to achieve your potential greatness? There is a unifying human story that makes sense of your personal story, one in which the details of our stories differ greatly, but the collective themes are common. C. S. Lewis described this story as the one true myth. *About You* picks up the threads of our shared story and weaves them progressively toward rediscovering what it means to be fully alive and fully human and then reveals the way to get there.

Remembering the Way We Were

In *About You* we will reflect on our collective memory of an earlier, better time and place. All of us experience human longing; we are wistful about what might have been. We intuitively sense that what we long for is something humans once possessed. It seems to us that there was a better time, a better place, where we experienced a deeper, more satisfying connection to the transcendent, to ourselves, to each other, and to the planet itself. This is one of the most common themes in music, poetry, fiction, and all art: "Once there was a way to get back homeward."

Reflecting on Our Diminishment

About You explores the dissonance between our memories of the way we were and the reality of the way we are. We yearn to be fully alive and fully human, but the very fact that we yearn for this means it is not an actuality. We want to be more than we are, but are somehow less than we should be. We want rich personal relationships, but sometimes feel isolated and alone. We feel less than fully human, which is another way of saying we have somehow been dehumanized. What went wrong and what can be done about it?

Rediscovering Fully Human

About You offers hope by illuminating the path to becoming fully alive and fully human. As my friend Nigel says, "We are not human doings, or human beings, we are human becomings!" To become fully alive and fully human requires coming to our senses, a returning and waking from the dead. These metaphors hint at a spiritual experience, but it is more than that. Some people live humanly but are lacking spiritually. Others aspire to be spiritual but aren't winsomely alive and human. We are looking for a way that fully integrates both: being fully alive spiritually and fully human.

Revealing the Way to Restoration

About You builds on the idea that our restoration is birthed at the intersection of anthropology (what is the nature and destiny of humans) and theology (what is the nature of God and what are God's purposes). Christians believe Jesus is the embodiment of this intersection, because he is described as fully God and fully man and claims to know the way to fully human and fully alive. But *About You* is not just for Christians, because Jesus came for all people everywhere.

The themes of this book flow from many streams, but there are three significant ones you should watch for, and taken together they lead to conclusions you will not read anywhere else. One answers the question: What can humans do to please God? St. Irenaeus answers saying, "The glory of God is man fully alive." The second answers the question: What was the mission of Jesus? Hans Rookmaaker answers saying, "Jesus didn't come to make us Christian; Jesus came to make us fully human." The third answers the question: What does fully human look like? The answer comes from my own understanding that regardless of nationality, ethnic origin, religion, or creed, each and every person on earth is a bearer of God's image creatively, spiritually, intelligently, morally, and relationally in ways unique to them.

If you get nothing else from this book, remember these three truths. (1) Being fully alive and fully human is God's original and continued intention for you; (2) God sent Jesus to rehumanize what has been dehumanized in all humans, including you; (3) God can restore you to your uniquely designed creative, spiritual, intelligent, moral, and relational self.

Come with me and explore the wonder of who you were made to be. See how the sheen of your brilliance can be restored. Discover how your unique design is the secret to finding your calling and destiny. Reach your fullest potential and become the best version of yourself. This book is about you—who you are now, who you want to become, and who you can become.

acknowledgments

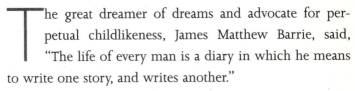

The great dreamer of dreams and advocate for perpetual childlikeness, James Matthew Barrie, said, "The life of every man is a diary in which he means to write one story, and writes another."

Left to my own devices, the life I would have lived would have been markedly different from the one I have actually lived and the book I have written could not have been written.

I want to acknowledge my parents and grandparents for contributing to me the genetic pool in which I swim.

Childhood friends like Jimmy Sellers, Pete Claudius, and Shawn Nolan bumped my trajectory in random ways with unforeseen consequences. My sisters Becky and Ruthy, and my brother Timmy from his wheelchair, altered my course by being who they are and being there.

Among my biggest influences were those hapless souls entrusted with my education, formally and informally, and memorable ones include Mrs. Duff, Mr. Baumann, Don Kenyon, Hugh Humphries, Elizabeth Hough, Russ Marshall, David and Jeanette Scholer, Glenn Barker, Bill Lane, Helmut Koester, Bishop Stephen Neill, John Stott, Martin Marty, Jerry Root, R. A. Harlan, and Rev. Earl Palmer.

My broadcasting career offered a graduate school education as each day I interviewed thoughtful, creative cultural influencers, luminaries, and unknowns. My bookshelves are lined with their contributions to my thinking, as I committed never to interview anyone whose book I had not read. (See sample guest list: http://www.dickstaub.com/display .php?section=About%20The%20Dick%20Staub%20Show.) Fellow sojourners who've influenced me along the way include Walt Mueller, Rob Johnston, Craig Detweiler, Mako Fujimura, Greg Wolfe, John Fischer, the Priddy Brothers, Neil Postman, Brennan Manning, and from a distance, C. S. Lewis and Hans Rookmaaker.

Along the way I've collected what could either be described as an odd assortment of friends, or an assortment of odd friends, whose presence has been at least entertaining, if not at times enlightening. They include but are not limited to Ray Homan, Dave and Nancy Carlstrom, Bob and Joy Drovdahl, Jack and Vicky Carney, Bob and Cindy Ward, Marty and Marcie O'Donnell, Nigel and Gillie Goodwin, Phill Butler, Ralph Mattson, Art Miller, Paul Ingram, Carlo Nakar, Lori Solyum, Jennie Spohr, everyone in the *Kindlings Movement* (see http://www.thekindlings.com), and all my friends on Orcas Island, not the least of whom are Grant Myles-Era and Scott Harris.

Special appreciation to Joe and Judy Rehfeld, Jim and Bev Ohlman, Terry and Corrie Moore, and Jack and Cynthia Talley for allowing me to use their getaway places for thinking and writing. Also a special appreciation for Jack and Alex McMillan, Ron and Nancy Nyberg, Jack and Sheri Hoover, and Greg and Kathy Strang for reasons they know all too well.

I love working with Torrey and everybody else at faceoutstudio on my book covers. Thanks again to Julianna, who brought me into the Jossey-Bass fold, and to Sheryl, Alison, Joanne, and so many others from Jossey-Bass for investing time and energy in this book.

I

human potential
and our universal
dilemma

1

you are a masterpiece

Most men lead lives of quiet desperation
and go to the grave with the song still in
them.

—THOREAU

Once upon a time an adolescent asked Mozart how
to compose symphonies. Because the lad was so
young, Mozart suggested that perhaps he should
begin by composing ballads. "But," the young man object-
ed, "you wrote symphonies when you were only ten years
old." Mozart replied, "But I didn't have to ask how."

There are two important lessons in this story. First,
Mozart was a genius (which can be defined as one with
exceptional natural capacity of intellect, especially as shown
in creative and original work in science, art, and music).

Second, Mozart was fortunate enough to have discovered his genius, and at a very young age.

But there is a third important lesson here, and this one is about you. Webster's second definition of *genius* is "an individual's natural abilities and capacities." In this sense, you are a genius! *About You* explores the origin of your genius and will help you discover your blend of unique talents, capacities, personality, and life experiences so that you can become the absolute best version of yourself.

I have always been intrigued by the powerful notion of individual genius, but the simplistic bromides of positive thinking have turned me off. This book takes the position that there is a factual basis for believing in your inestimable worth: you are created by an infinitely creative God. It also takes seriously the obstacles to achieving your potential and concludes that you cannot achieve it by yourself, but the good news is help is available.

I know, you don't need another book. It's not as if there aren't enough books out there already, sitting lonely and forlorn, stacked high in bedrooms and offices, unread. It's not as if you have a lot of extra time to read another one, busy as you are with whatever you are busy with: work, a love life, raising kids, watching reruns of *Friends* or *Gilligan's Island*, Tweeting, game playing, movie watching, Facebooking, scrapbooking—any one of which leave little time for book reading.

Even book lovers agree. Ecclesiastes got it right, "Of making many books there is no end, and much study wearies the body."

And yet you purchased this slim volume or loaded its electronic version onto your e-reader. Why this book? What made you pick it up, turn it over, read the back cover, carry it to a cashier, or click and order it through an online bookseller?

You don't need another book but you wanted this one, probably because it is about something that matters to you: you and your desire to live a fuller and more complete life, to become fully human.

You are not alone in your quest. Throughout the centuries, thinking humans, whether mere mortals, philosophers, prophets, or sages, have asked the same universal questions: What is a human being? Who am I? Why am I here? What is the meaning and significance of human life, and my life specifically?

Most ancient philosophers believed the primary job of the philosopher was to answer the questions: How do people live happy, fulfilling lives and how can they be good persons? There has been no shortage of verbiage on these matters: Know thyself. To thine own self be true. The unexamined life is not worth living. The chief end of man is to glorify God and to enjoy Him forever.

Experiencing a satisfying life requires answering these questions for yourself, and consciously or not from the very beginning you've been naturally curious about your place in the world. When you first emerged from your mother's womb, your journey of self-discovery and wonder began.

As a newborn you got in touch with yourself, literally—your fingers and toes, your hunger pangs, your pain,

your discomfort. Soon your eyes became a portal of discovery to a world beyond yourself and your ears began to
capture the exotic, mysterious sounds of others. *What is that?*
Who is that? What have they to do with me? Your crawling
turned to walking, your indistinguishable blabber turned
to talking, and one day you became the reader of bedtime
stories instead of the listener.

The infant became a child, the child became a teen,
the teen became an adult and an immense, complex world
unfolded before you as the curious explorer who, though
but a speck of dust trapped in time, began searching for
meaning, wisdom, and maybe even for the eternal, transcendent God.

Your solitary journey commenced with a sense of
limitless possibilities and an expansive awareness of your
own potential. Soon you were joined by family, friends,
neighbors, acquaintances, the media, teachers, and a million other external influences who set about their work of
expanding your sense of value and worth or diminishing
it, of constructively guiding or derailing you, of clarifying
your life's purpose or diverting you from it.

Perhaps your life has unfolded ideally and just as you
planned. But for most of us, life deals some serious blows
and detours. Paraphrasing Tolstoy, happy humans are all
alike, but every unhappy human is unhappy in his or her
own way. You didn't make the team or you made the team
but didn't play, or you played a lot but on a losing team,
or you played on the championship team but still didn't
feel like a winner. You didn't get cast in the play or you got
cast but in a minor role; you weren't chosen for the select

band or choir; you scored too low on the SATs; you weren't admitted to the college of your choice; your one true love broke your heart, leaving you for another; your parents divorced; you were passed by for the job of your dreams and have languished in lesser work, or you got the job of your dreams and hated it. You finished school or were well into your career before you realized that you didn't really know what you wanted to be when you grew up!

Privately you've written poems or songs that no one will ever hear or drawn sketches or created art no one will ever see. This saddens you because this deeply personal work somehow reflects the essential you, the one longing for expression, hungry to be known. Some folks' lives roll easily and sometimes yours never seems to roll at all. Life batters and shatters you and one day you wake up fearing you are becoming the person described in Thoreau's haunting refrain: "Most men lead lives of quiet desperation and go to the grave with the song still in them."

You wonder if you've missed your own life the way someone misses a plane. You ask: Has it taken a lifetime or did it happen overnight that I become a hollowed-out version of the person I might have become? "The greatest hazard of all, losing one's self, can occur very quietly in the world, as if it were nothing at all. No other loss can occur so quietly; any other loss—an arm, a leg, five dollars, a wife, etc.—is sure to be noticed." So said the wistful and wise Danish philosopher Søren Kierkegaard in his masterpiece *Sickness Unto Death*.

And so I have written this little book to share what I've learned about becoming fully human. I've studied this question academically, completing graduate studies with a concentration in the humanities (philosophy, the arts, religion), because, after all, the humanities are the study of humans and the culture they create, and that is what I was interested in.

I've sought the answers to life's deepest questions personally, through trial and error, successes and failures. My philosophical quest began in earnest when I was ten years old and my brother Timmy was born with brain damage, leaving him unable to walk, talk, feed, or care for himself. My childlike trust in God unraveled and my questions about the nature and meaning of human existence were born. Did my brother's life have meaning? What was a fully human life and could he ever live one?

As an adult I've traveled to more than fifty countries, listening to and observing the universal, common desires of all humans, seeking to understand how we are alike instead of focusing on the differences that so often divide us.

My career took me into a large corporate, then nonprofit, environment where I rose through the ranks of management only to discover that my work was a good use of my talents, but not the best use.

A Few Lessons I've Learned

Perhaps my greatest education in our subject came as a broadcaster where, as a nationally syndicated talk show host, I was afforded a unique vantage point from which to understand people's hopes, dreams, aspirations, disappointments, sorrows, and frustrations. For fifteen years my daily life consisted of reading five newspapers a day, devouring thirty journals a month, and then identifying and evaluating contemporary trends in light of ancient wisdom. On a show billed as a home for warm hearts, active minds, and hungry souls, during three hours each day I interviewed influential authors and talked with callers about ideas that matter. Although occasionally I heard upbeat answers from callers and guests, more often I heard tales of lives unraveling and hopes gone unfulfilled.

Let me underscore a few themes that I've learned.

Most People Can and Should Live Fuller Lives and Will Be Chronically Unhappy If They Don't

Full means complete in all respects. Applied to humans, living fully means living a complete life as opposed to an incomplete, partial, or compartmentalized life. The ancient Greeks called this complete life *arête*, a word used to describe the lives of people who had reached their fullest potential. Fame or wealth was not the measure of such a life. Rather these individuals aspired to become well-rounded persons: physically, mentally, morally, and spiritually. The Greeks understood that each individual's unique capacities—or "genius"—enabled him or her to excel at certain aspects of life over others, but they believed the full life involved the total development of the whole person.

This same thought is captured in the Hebrew word *shalom*, which is generally translated into English as "peace" but actually refers less to the cessation of war than to whole-ness and well-being. To achieve *shalom* means to arrive at a balanced, healthy, and whole life.

The Greeks and Hebrews assumed that achieving less than a full, complete, and balanced life leaves one with a sense of incompleteness and an acute awareness that some-thing is missing. Does this not describe most contemporary humans?

Many People Have Forgotten the Magnificence of Being Human and Have Little Sense of Their Unique, Extraordinary Potential

We aim for fullness and completeness, but what does it mean to be fully *human?* What differentiates humans from animals? Even today's most rigorous materialist would say humans are distinguishable by our intellectual, creative, moral, relational, and even spiritual capacities. Might it be that we today are dissatisfied with our lives because we have lost touch with these basic qualities of humanness itself? Is it possible that the way to a satisfactory and fulfilling life begins with rediscover-ing the essence of what it means to be human?

Psychologists generally agree that the happy life is the fully integrated life, not the compartmentalized life. They seek to make us well by helping us become emotionally whole, because anything less will result in a feeling of dis-satisfaction and a longing for something more. Academics develop the intellect, the religiously devout a spiritual life, athletes the body, artists the creative. What if being human involves all of these together, not the development of one or two in isolation from the others?

Most People Are Not Fully Alive

Most of us exist but are dispirited, indifferent, lacking in passion. This is a global phenomenon.

Sooner or later most humans realize that gone are the days of childhood when they were exuberant, alert, animated, hopeful, full of energy, and vivid and vibrant. Something important is missing, they realize, and they face a choice: give up, or try to fill the empty space. Those who haven't given up pursue learning, reading the wisdom of the ages, buying self-help books, or taking seminars. They meditate or turn to religion or a spiritual tradition or crawl onto the psychiatrist's couch. Those who have given up overmedicate, overeat, shop compulsively, drink too much, party too much, or find diversions through senseless entertainments and amusements.

About You

I am striving to become more fully alive and fully human, but this book is about you because I want you to join me in this quest.

Whether you are trying to fill the empty space or have already given up, *About You* is your invitation to an adventure that combines ancient wisdom and new insights. Together we will see that you have unique and incalculable value and worth; there is a reason you feel loss and longing and there is a path toward becoming fully alive and fully human. There is a grand and noble collective human story of which your life is a part, and your fulfillment and happiness depends on your living your unique story fully. There is within you an "inner Mozart" waiting to come out, and I want to help release it!

One final note as we get started on this journey together. Chaucer said, "A pilgrimage can be a rowdy affair." Given what I know about people and suspect to be true about you (my readers tend to march to the beat of a different drummer), I say, "Let your rowdy pilgrimage to fully human begin!"

II

primal humans

*the collective memory
of the way we were*

2

created

Talking about cosmology, you can't help
making the connection to religion. In all
religions, all cultures, there's always, "In
the beginning." Either you started from
something or you didn't, right?
—GEORGE SMOOT

Everything I know about becoming fully alive and
fully human starts with a simple but profoundly
important idea: God created humans and God created
us in the image of God so we can enjoy a rich intellectual,
creative, relational, moral, and spiritual life. You are not the
accidental result of a random, purposeless process but, in
fact, were created by a loving, personal God who had you
in mind before the beginning of time. This is an essential
and reasonable but embattled truth.

I am not a scientist, but I live in a scientific age. I am not a scientist, but I've always taken the natural world seriously. As I child I walked down the dirt road in Bly, Oregon, and watched Dayton Hyde observing the migratory pattern of a Sandhill Crane. He later wrote the book *Sandy, the Sand Hill Crane*. As a nine-year-old I stood under the starry sky and watched *Sputnik* fly overhead, and a few years later joined an astronomy club that met at Knott's Berry Farm and began work on a homemade telescope.

As a ten-year-old, inspired by Teddy Roosevelt, I opened my first Natural Wildlife Museum, complete with exhibits including a coyote skull, owl's wing, bobcat skin, ant farm, and a horned toad lizard live and in captivity. If you paid your five cents you could join the neighborhood kids lined up around the block to gain entrance to this wonder of the world, with all profits used to fund future expeditions into the wild by the renowned adventurer Sir Richard Staub.

In college I sat in front of a small TV screen mesmerized by the crew of *Apollo 11* and watched Neil Armstrong step onto the surface of the moon and utter those memorable words, "That's one small step for man, one giant leap for mankind."

As a broadcaster I've interviewed leading scientists including George Smoot, astrophysicist, cosmologist, and Nobel laureate in physics; Rocky Kolb, chair of the Department of Astronomy and Astrophysics at the University of Chicago; Michio Kaku, a Japanese American theoretical physicist specializing in string field theory; Francis Collins, head of the Human Genome Project; British particle physicist and theologian John Polkinghorne; and many others.

If one pillar of my life has been a fascination with the natural world, the other has been my pursuit of the spiritual. I have never doubted the existence of a metaphysical world and neither of these interests has diminished my belief in the reality and importance of both.

By way of introduction I simply want you to know that I am serious about both my faith *and* contemporary science. I think they are compatible. I do not believe issues of apparent disagreement between faith and science can be resolved by ignoring or dismissing one or the other; rather, we need to see them as equally important albeit different ways of looking at the same world.

In this chapter I want to affirm your confidence that God is your creator. If you do not believe in God, or believe in God but one uninvolved in creation, this short chapter cannot possibly change your mind, nor is it intended to. But God's involvement in creation is a starting point and a dividing point in understanding the truth about you.

You Are Created by God—an Essential and Empowering Truth

From the beginning of recorded history, humans believed in the reality of both the physical and spiritual worlds. The earliest oral and then written traditions always included some explanation for the creation of the planet and its inhabitants. The most familiar ancient account of creation is recorded in the biblical creation story, which opens dramatically with the provocative words, "In the beginning, God created."

The ancient stories did not attempt to prove the existence of God because God's existence was assumed to be obvious. The biblical account teaches that the God who exists reveals certain insights enabling us to understand the spiritual world and its connection to the physical. Jews and Christians believe the Bible is a written revelation of truths disclosed by God to humans who faithfully and accurately wrote down what God revealed to them.

The opening verse in the Bible reveals first that God exists (*In the beginning, God* ...) and second that God created (*In the beginning, God created* ...). The biblical creation story progressively builds from the creation of the heavens and earth, to the creation of light, land, vegetation, living creatures in the water and sky, and land-bound livestock, and finally to the creation of man and woman. We are told that humans are the pinnacle of creation and were "made just a little lower than the angels."

Today, Christians agree that God is creator, but they disagree about the specifics of creation. There are dozens of explanations for how God created, from the young earth, six-day literal creation story to the theistic evolution story, which propounds that evolution is a tool God employed to develop human life. Although Christians disagree on the how of God's involvement in creation, they all agree on the who: in the beginning God created, and all created things are the result of God's creative work.

The ancients took the biblical creation story very seriously and saw the implications of the creator's ongoing involvement in their personal lives. In the early Jewish documents we read, "Your hands shaped me and made me. The Spirit of God has made me; the breath of the Almighty gives me life." The psalmist wrote, "For you created my inmost being; you knit me together in my mother's womb. All the days ordained for me were written in your book before one of them came to be." The prophet Jeremiah declared, "For I know the plans I have for you. . . . plans to prosper you and not to harm you, plans to give you hope and a future."

By the first century A.D. the apostle Paul, a Jewish philosopher, theologian, and early Christian convert, declared that the entire universe would spin apart were it not for the creative, sustaining presence of God. He said of Jesus, "He is the image of the invisible God, the firstborn over all creation. For by him all things were created: things in heaven and on earth, visible and invisible, whether thrones or powers or rulers or authorities; all things were created by him and for him. He is before all things, and *in him all things hold together.*"

The belief that God created the universe and is still involved in human existence has been an empowering one through the centuries. Because of the creation story we humans have understood ourselves to be the result of a creative, purposeful, and personal God who has endowed us with extraordinary capacities and special responsibilities. I agree.

An Embattled Truth

Throughout history there have also been those who believe there is no such thing as spirit, the spiritual, or an unseen God. Some ancient Greek philosophers theorized that the world consists of four elements—fire, water, earth, and air—and that everything in it arose by natural process and chance.

During the Enlightenment (the seventeenth and eighteenth centuries) philosophers took on the subject of *how we know* what we know (what philosophers call *epistemology*). Many of them drew clear lines between knowledge verified with proof and religious knowledge, which requires faith and belief because it cannot provide indisputable material proof. Thus began a subtle diminishment of religious knowledge as an inferior way of knowing. In the 1800s the materialistic view gained momentum with the ideas of Charles Darwin, who theorized that all of creation is the result of an unguided, unplanned process of random variation and natural selection. Though most aspects of his theories did not require the abandonment of belief in God as creator, Darwin eventually rejected his belief in God as creator, concluding that there is no intentional, purposeful, intelligent deity and that humans do not occupy any special preordained role on earth. From that point forward, evolutionists have been divided into those who believe in God and those who don't; those who believe God was involved in creation and those who think every aspect of creation has been the result of random, unintentional, unplanned processes.

Darwin understood the radical consequences of his atheistic conclusions. In his 1838 notebooks, he wrote that there is no special place for humans. "Man in his arrogance thinks himself a great work, worthy of the interposition of a Deity. More humble and, I believe, true to consider him created from animals." Darwin also understood that his materialistic world absent God eliminated the idea of a universal moral code, saying, "One can have for his rule of life, as far as I can see, only to follow those impulses and instincts which are the strongest or which seem to him the best ones." Darwin concluded that contrary to biblical accounts human free will is an illusion. All of our actions, our thoughts, and intentions are the result of our "hereditary constitution" or "the example . . . or teaching of others."[1]

Ultimately Darwin's view of a world without God eliminated any hope for a meaningful, purposeful life. To summarize Darwin, he concluded that all human behavior can be explained by genetics, so that art, religion, alcoholism, sexual preference or addictions, violence, morality, human thoughts and their expression, are nothing more than accidental by-products of organisms swimming randomly in the experimental Petri dish of planet earth.

Many in the scientific community are perpetuating these atheistic evolutionist views today.

Francis Crick, one of the co-discoverers of the molecular structure of the genetic molecule, DNA, famously quipped, "You, your joys and your sorrows, your memories and your ambitions, your sense of personal identity and free will, are in fact no more than the behavior of a vast assembly of nerve cells and their associated molecules."[2]

Biologist Bruce Albert, former president of the National Academy of the Sciences, points out the devastating implications of this theory for humans: "In the last ten years we have come to realize humans are more like worms than we ever imagined. Genetically speaking, the worm represents a very simple human."[3] Some materialists like philosopher Daniel Dennett understand the ultimate consequences of atheistic materialism, saying, "Darwinism functions like a 'universal acid,' destroying traditional forms of religion and morality."[4]

Such views are alive and well today; they are the underlying factor in the "whatever," nihilistic perspective on life. The implications of atheistic, mechanistic evolution have worked their way into popular culture in books like *Fight Club*, where Tyler Darden announces, "You are not a beautiful or unique snowflake. You're the same organic matter as everyone else and we are all part of the same compost pile."[5] People who believe they are animals somehow feel more justified when they behave like animals. After all, what meaning does life hold for us if we are nothing but complex worms? If life has no deeper meaning, who cares about life? If God is not your creator then there is no use talking about your uniqueness as one created in God's image, no spiritual explanation for what seem to be your soul's longings.

These are not comforting views, but we don't seek comfort; we seek the truth even if it is uncomfortable. I do not choose to believe God is the creator because this belief comforts me; I believe it because it is true! And because this issue is so important, and the truth of God as your creator is so embattled, it is essential that you understand that the idea that God is your creator is a revealed, reliable, and reasonable truth.

A Revealed Truth

Although the Bible was written over the period of a few thousand years by multiple authors in different languages and places, the creation story and its implications are consistent from the first pages of the Bible to the last. The writer of Hebrews reminds us that long ago God spoke to our ancestors in many and various ways through the prophets, but in these last days he spoke to us through a Son, whom he appointed "heir of all things, through whom he also created the worlds." God's role as your creator is a fundamental and essential teaching of the Bible.

Even if you don't rely on biblical revelation for discovering truth, nature itself reveals the truth of a creator. The psalmist observed, "The heavens are telling the glory of God." The apostle Paul concluded that God's revelation through creation is clear: the extraordinary created order itself is enough to prove that there is a creator behind it. "Since the creation of the world, God's invisible qualities—his eternal power and divine nature—have been clearly seen, being understood from what has been made, so that men are without excuse." The materialist sees creation only as the sum of its parts, whereas the theist sees every aspect of creation pointing to a magnificent creator. Poets, novelists, songwriters, artists, and filmmakers see the imaginative drama and theater of the created world; the materialist misses the transcendent inspiration.

It has been said of England and the United States that we are two countries separated by a common language. Similarly, when it comes to faith and science we often look at the same thing but see it very differently. A simple story illustrates the point. A music major and her science major boyfriend were taking a romantic walk on a beautiful evening. While the sounds of crickets surrounded them, the music major heard the lilting voices of a church choir off in the distance. She said of the choir, "Isn't that sound beautiful?" The boyfriend, thinking of the crickets, replied, "Yes, and isn't it amazing that they make that sound by rubbing their hind legs together?" The belief in a creator has resonated in the human heart for centuries. This is why the appetite for the transcendent has been found in every human culture throughout history. Tribal and ethnic traditions and ancient myths all hint at a creator God and each tells a creation story that gives evidence of a belief in and quest for the transcendent. This is one reason why, despite the dominance of Darwinist thought, people everywhere, including in the Western world, still believe in God and God's involvement in creation.

A Reasonable Truth

Scripture, nature, and the human heart all reveal the existence of a creator God, and today many scientists confirm that this belief is reasonable because our study of the universe is revealing an immensity, complexity, and underlying orderliness that is best explained by the existence of God.

Back in the 1990s George Smoot, Nobel Prize laureate in physics, offended the scientific community when on the TV show *Nightline* he explained the big bang theory and added that what we are seeing through this theory is "like seeing the hand of God." Later, during an interview on my radio show, I asked him why he mentioned God in his discussion of the big bang. He said, "I invoked God because it's a cultural icon people understand—but there's something deeper. Talking about cosmology, you can't help making the connection to religion. In all religions, all cultures, there's always, 'In the beginning.' Either you started from something or you didn't, right?"[6]

Science can make truly great progress in the study of the material world, but it is of little value in examining spiritual, nonmaterial reality. A. N. Wilson, who was once an atheist, recently returned to the Christian faith in part because he realized that "materialist atheism says we are just a collection of chemicals. It has no answer whatsoever to the question of how we should be capable of love or heroism or poetry if we are simply animated pieces of meat."[7] Those who believe in God believe physical reality came into being through one who transcends and precedes the material world. The honest scientist will admit that scientific methodology cannot prove or disprove the existence of an immaterial first cause.

This seemed painfully obvious in the movie *Expelled*, when Ben Stein interviewed Richard Dawkins, scientist and leading proponent of atheism. Challenged to explain an alternative to the origin of life itself Dawkins stammered, stumbled, and then suggested life possibly came to earth from another planet. He said, "At some earlier time somewhere in the universe a civilization evolved, probably by some kind of Darwinian means, to a very, very high level of technology and designed a form of life that they seeded onto . . . perhaps this . . . this planet." Dawkins's answer, of course, raises a new question, which is: What was the origin of this mysterious, unknown advanced civilization that was capable of seeding our own planet with a well-designed form of life?

The discovery and mapping of DNA has revealed a complexity that many say dismisses random chance as a plausible explanation for DNA. They argue that it is statistically and mathematically impossible. What are the odds that a free-living, single-celled organism, such as a bacterium, might result by the chance combining of preexistent building blocks? Atheistic physicist Harold Morowitz calculated the odds as one chance in $10^{100,000,000,000}$ (that is, ten to the one hundred billionth power). Sir Fred Hoyle calculated the odds of just the proteins of an amoeba arising by chance as one in $10^{40,000}$ (ten to the forty thousandth power).

To help us understand these numbers, Mark Eastman, author of *Creation by Design*, says that Morowitz's calculation means "it is more likely that I would win the state lottery every week for a million years by purchasing just one ticket each week than it is that DNA developed by chance. The odds led Fred Hoyle to state that the probability of spontaneous generation 'is about the same as the probability that a tornado sweeping through a junkyard could assemble a Boeing 747 from the contents therein.' Mathematicians tell us that any event with an improbability greater than one chance in 10^{50} is in the realm of metaphysics—i.e., a miracle."[8]

When we recognize the proper and limited roles of both science and theology, what we are learning about the universe strengthens the reasonableness of believing there is an intelligent creator. Science is not able to address metaphysical, spiritual realities, and the Bible is not a science textbook. Taken together and properly understood and interpreted, faith and science point in the same direction: to an extraordinary created order with a first cause beyond our comprehension.

There is a burgeoning breed of scientists intent on researching the physical imprint of the spiritual, which points toward the reality of the unseen.[9] Might we be entering a new Enlightenment that allows us to explore creation's complexity while at the same time honoring and reverencing the creator of this universe who created humans in His image? As the scientific community receives data revealing something real that transcends the realm of scientific measurability, we may be approaching a paradigm shift in which faith and science are both respected as different ways of viewing the same reality—with each performing an essential function.

We should respect the facts of our human uniqueness, including our spiritual capacity. As philosopher Robert Sokolowski recently observed: "It is a curious thing that human beings spend so much energy denying their own spiritual and rational nature. No other being tries with such effort to deny that it is what it is. No dog or horse would ever try to show that it is not a dog or horse but only a mixture of matter, force, and accident. Man's attempt to deny his own spirituality is itself a spiritual act, one that transcends space, time, and the limitations of matter. The motivations behind this self-denial are mystifying indeed."[10]

This book is about you and your pilgrimage toward being fully human. The starting point of this journey is believing that there is a God and that God is your creator. You are not the result of a random, unplanned, unguided process. God's involvement and intentionality in your creation have been revealed in the words of Scripture, in your heart, and in the world, and therefore it is reasonable to proceed confidently in the knowledge that you are special, unique, and loved by the God who created you. Better yet, as you will read in the next chapter, you are created in God's image.

3

in god's image

> It was a number of years of crashing and
> burning before I made the discovery that
> I was not God. Finally I realized that
> though I was not God, I was of God.
>
> —NEVADA BARR

You are godlike, but you are not God.

In the movie *Malice*, Alex Baldwin plays Dr. Jed Hill, a brilliant surgeon who has confused his godlikeness for God. Facing a lawsuit for a decision he made in the operating room, he goes to great lengths to confirm his infallibility. During a legal deposition he talks about his stellar academic credentials, multiple awards, and untarnished reputation.

He asks who families are praying to when they go to the hospital chapel, and then answers that if they are praying for a patient in his operating room, they are praying to him, adding, "You ask me if I have a God complex? Let me tell you something: I am God." Thus we come to the old joke: What is the difference between a surgeon and God? The answer, God doesn't think He's a surgeon.

Our confusion about whether or not we are God arises from the fact that although we are *not* God we are *like* God. Our godlikeness is described in the first chapter of the Bible. Genesis 1:26–27 reveals, "Then God said, 'Let us make man in our image, in our likeness, and let him rule over the fish of the sea and the birds of the air, over the livestock, over all the earth, and over all the creatures that move along the ground.' So God created man in his own image, in the image of God he created him; male and female he created them."

Imago Dei: You Are a Snapshot of God

What does it mean to be created in God's image? The Hebrew root of the Latin phrase for image of God—*imago Dei*—means image, shadow, or likeness of God. You are a snapshot or facsimile of God. At the very least this means humans occupy a higher place in the created order because we alone are imprinted with godlike characteristics. Your godlikeness is the path to your greatest fulfillment. You will feel the greatest pleasure and wholeness when who God made you to be is fully developed and expressed.

In *Chariots of Fire* Eric Lidell is torn between his call to be a missionary to China and his passion for running. He explains the dilemma to his sister by saying that God called him to be a missionary, but God also made him to run fast, and when he runs he feels God's pleasure.

Your godlikeness can also be a pitfall, because in our hubris we often confuse being like God with being God. Mystery writer Nevada Barr learned this after returning to faith from her long sojourn on the wild side, and concluded, "It was a number of years of crashing and burning before I made the discovery that I was not God. Finally I realized that though I was not God, I was of God."[1]

Even if you don't believe in God or are irreligious, what the Bible teaches is true: God's imprint on your life never leaves you. There are those who have ceased to believe in God, yet are haunted by the realization that though they wander far from God, God's image goes with them. Even the atheist bears God's image.

God's imprint is on your life even when it is no longer outwardly evident. In the New Testament story of the prodigal son a young man squanders his potential and hits bottom, bereft of the beauty and promise he once possessed. Yet the point of the story is that the father still sees and appreciates the worth of his wayward son.

About You and Your Godlike Aptitudes

But in what *way* are you an image of God? How are you godlike? Theologians have long debated this question, but the answer becomes clear when we read the description of

God in Genesis 1 and then ask: If we could take a snapshot of God what would we see and what would it reveal about humans created in God's image?

First, the truth about you is that *you are creative* because God is creative: *In the beginning God created the heavens and the earth* (Genesis 1:1). We know that God is creative, or as my friend Nigel Goodwin says, "God is the great artist!" Not everyone is an artist, but every human makes things. Artists make things with paint. Poets, writers, philosophers, and lawyers make things with ideas and the compelling use of words. Composers use notes to make music; choirs do it with their voices and orchestras do it with their instruments. Doctors make people healthier; consultants make organizations better. Manufacturers make things with raw materials; chefs make things with fruits, vegetables, meats, and spices. Every human has the capacity to make things, to create, because we are all made in the image of a creative God. Dorothy Sayers once observed that if all we knew about God was Genesis 1:1 then all we would know is that God is creative.[2] But of course that is not all we know about God. Genesis 1 reveals other qualities of God, and because we are a snapshot of God, they give us glimpses into who we are as those made in God's image.

The second truth about you is that you are *spiritual* because God is Spirit: *The Spirit of God was hovering over the waters* (Genesis 1:2). Every human possesses spiritual aptitudes and capacities. We are more than the sum of our physical parts. Our spiritual nature, though unseen, is as real as our physical nature. Nurturing our spirit is as important as eating, drinking, and exercising are to our physical body. We are spiritual beings having a human experience, and to be fully human means to be spiritual.

A third truth about you is that you *communicate* because God communicates: *God said, "Let there be light"* (Genesis 1:3). Anthropologists agree that the emergence of symbolic language—first spoken, then written—represents the sharpest break between animals and humans. The human ability to think and reason, to use language, symbols, and art, far surpasses the abilities of any animals. This gift was bestowed when the communicative God's image was imprinted on us. In the Biblical story words are important. The world is created when God says the word and Jesus himself is described as the word.

A fourth truth about you is that you are *intelligent* because God is intelligent: in the beginning was the Word (*logos*, a Greek word meaning reason, or logic) and the Word was with God, and the Word was God (John 1:1). Logical sequential thought flows from the orderliness of God's mind. As a result, though we are not all intellectuals, we each possess a mind and a way of thinking and learning, so Jesus commanded us to love God with our minds (as well as our hearts and all our strength). Because of God's intelligent image imprinted on our lives, though we possess different kinds of intelligence, each of us is to develop our mental capacities to their fullest. Thinking is not an optional choice available to scholars and the elite; thinking is an essential characteristic of being human.

A fifth truth about you is that you are *relational* because God is relational: *Let us make man in our image, in our likeness.*

It is not good for man to be alone (Genesis 1:27). Amazingly,
the phrase, "Let us make man in our image" reveals an
"us-ness" in the very nature of God. The very essence of God
is relational, and that essential quality has been imprinted
on humans. Jewish theologian Martin Buber concluded
that our primary relationship is with the transcendent God.
He called this an I-Thou relationship because God is not
an idea or an object or an "it" but rather a person who is
known relationally. This capacity for a relationship with
God extends to humans, which is why the Genesis story
declares that God created Eve for Adam because "it is not
good for man to be alone."

A sixth truth about you is that you are *morally responsible* because God is a moral being. And the Lord God
commanded the man, "You are free to eat from any tree
in the garden; but you must not eat from the tree of the
knowledge of good and evil, for when you eat of it you
will surely die" (Genesis 2:16–17). Just as there are natural
laws that govern the universe, universal moral laws govern
human behavior. The Bible teaches that these laws are written on human hearts and are universal, transcending any
particular religion. C. S. Lewis intentionally draws from the
Confucian tradition in calling this universal code the *Tao* to
show that authorities from different times and places all
agree that embracing the good, the true, and the beautiful is
fundamental for happy human living. This Tao, the universal
moral code, is not the private property of an individual,
group, religion, or civilization, but common to all, perma-
nent and real. In the biblical creation story this universal

moral nature originates in God's image imprinted on each human at creation.

Finally the creation story reveals that you are *purposeful* because God is purposeful. At creation God gave humans a purpose. God blessed them and said to them, "Be fruitful and increase in number; fill the earth and subdue it. Rule over the fish of the sea and the birds of the air and over every living creature that moves on the ground" (Genesis 1:28). Immediately after God created them, humans set about to fulfill this specific purpose, beginning by naming the animals.

When we fully grasp what it means to bear God's image, we are at once struck with the grandeur of our possibilities and the tragedy of our unrealized potential. To be fully human is to fully reflect God's creative, spiritual, intelligent, communicative, relational, moral, and purposeful capacities, and to do so holistically and synergistically. Furthermore, though all humans possess these godlike capacities, each of us has the potential to express them distinctively, because God's image has been imprinted uniquely on each of us. In God's infinite creativity there are no duplicates; you are the *only* you there has ever been or ever will be.

Only One You

Attaining a fully human life requires you not only to know the general ways in which you are like God and other humans but also to know and express what is specifically unique about you. Though all humans share the same dynamic cluster of capacities, you are a unique blend, a custom mix of talents, temperament, and personality.

Eighteenth-century artist Francisco Goya invented a hat with candles mounted on it so he could paint at night. He then painted a self-portrait with the hat, lit candles and all, perched precariously on his head. Today, we look at the painting and ask what possessed him to create such a thing. Was it whimsy? Was it madness? Was it genius? Was it individuality? Was it artistic obsession? Was it all of these and more? In today's conformist society the artist Goya stands out inspirationally as a man who knew who he was and what he wanted and then expressed it all in his work—and even in his hat. Poet laureate Billy Collins's poem *Goya's Hat* captures what fascinates me, observing that once you've seen the hat you know all you need to know about Goya. You no longer need to know the dates he lived or even to read his biography. The hat tells the story of the essential uniqueness of the man!

Socrates said, "Know yourself," and Shakespeare added, "To your own self be true." There is a unique, rich genius locked in every human soul, a "you-ness," an inner Goya, that transcends genome and defies comparison. This inner you began to manifest itself during your childhood. Think of the boldness of children and the outrageous, unselfconscious acts they perform before learning to behave more conventionally. The sparks that fly in childhood will either be fanned to flame or tamped out. Sparks grow from the inside and need air and space to grow into fire. Too much external tampering can put out that iridescent flame. In his book *Orbiting the Giant Hairball*, Gordon MacKenzie tells of how he visited classrooms to share his art. At the beginning of each class he always asked how many of the students were artists. In kindergarten every hand went up. By first grade maybe two-thirds of the kids said they were artists, by second grade maybe half. By middle school two kids raised their hands—the kids with purple hair and nose rings. Gordon's point was that years of sitting in straight rows and focusing on reading and math had tamped out the creative spark these kids originally possessed.

How are you unique and how will you express the brilliant reflection of you? For your life to blaze with your intended glory you must believe you are the only you and then discover, develop, and express the singular uniqueness that is already in you.

But it is important to realize that God, who created you as a unique individual, has also foreordained that your individualism will flourish within community with God and others. For life to be lived fully it must be lived together, not alone.

4

together

I had to have company—I was made for it,
I think.

—*EVE'S DIARY*

Humorist Mark Twain thought everything was fine in the Garden of Eden until Eve arrived.[1]

God disagreed.

In one of his most brilliant satirical pieces, *Extracts from Adam's Diary*, Twain has Adam complaining nonstop about "the new creature," Eve. She eats too much fruit and he fears that because of her they will run out of it. She goes outside in all weather, even fog. And she talks. "It used to be so pleasant and quiet here," he mutters.

Whimsically, Adam worries that "she has taken up with the snake now." She trusts all the animals, thinking that since she won't betray them they won't betray her either. When a mighty brontosaurus comes stomping into camp she regards it as an acquisition while Adam sees it as a calamity. How different these two humans are in almost every way!

God agreed with Twain that there was a problem in the garden, but made it clear that the problem was not Eve, but rather, Adam *without* Eve. God saw all that He had made and said it was good, except for one thing: "It is not good for the man to be alone. I will make a helper suitable for him" (Genesis 2:18).

Twain himself came to agree with God on this matter because he enjoyed an extraordinarily happy marriage with his devoted wife Livy, so he wrote a companion piece to *Extracts from Adam's Diary* titled *Eve's Diary*. Written the year after his wife's death, it ends touchingly with an epitaph to Livy, "Wherever she was, *there* was Eden."

In her diary Eve expresses her complaints about Adam, who seemed to her more interested in resting than anything else. He looked like a reptile, and he dumped on her the daunting task of naming all the animals. But when she discovered he could talk, she felt a new interest in him, adding, "For I love to talk." More importantly Twain's Eve possesses an awareness of something essential to human nature, "I *had* to have company—I was made for it, I think."

A Companionship Rooted in the Nature of God

Twain is reminding us that our essential need for company counterbalances our undeniable individuality. We thrive on camaraderie and companionship as much as or more than we crave occasional solitude. This too is the result of our creation in God's image, for the essence of God is togetherness. Within the person of God is an eternal perfected relationship, and as a result, made in God's image, humans desire to be together and to have reliable companions and friends.

In the first chapter of Genesis we read, "God said, 'Let us' make humans in our own image" (Genesis 1:26). God's reference to "us" seems odd here for it implies that more than one God is present at creation, yet Christianity, as well as the Judaism from which it derives, has always been monotheistic. Christians believe in one God. As a boy Jesus prayed the Jewish *shema*, "Hear, O Israel, the Lord our God is one." How do we explain the apparent contradiction between the "us" involved in creation and the belief in one God?

The answer is that the Bible reveals a radical, paradoxical mystery, namely that there is one God who exists in three persons—God the Father, God the Son, and God the Holy Spirit.

> In the beginning *God* created the heavens and the
> earth and the *Spirit* hovered over the waters (Genesis
> 1:1–2). In the beginning was the Word and the
> Word was with God and the Word was God.
> *The Word (Jesus)* was with God in the beginning.
> Through him all things were made; without him
> nothing was made that has been made (John 1:1–2).

This mysterious union of one God in three persons is called the Trinity, the paradoxical Christian belief that one God exists eternally in perfect synergistic harmony in three persons—Father, Son, and Holy Spirit—and that there is community and collaboration within the very person of God.

God is a self-contained, eternal episode of *Friends*. "Let us" is a continuous reminder that we are created by a relational God who experiences in oneness a constant camaraderie of three persons. Within the Triune (three in one) God is the dynamic, relational expression of His attributes: creative, communicative, wise, infinite, sovereign, holy, all-knowing, faithful, self-existent, self-sufficient, just, unchanging, merciful, eternal, good, gracious, and always present. God is love and within God is the highest expression of perfect, self-giving, other-centered love. Where there is the Spirit of the Lord there is peace, laughter, joy, patience, kindness, generosity, faithfulness, gentleness, and self-control. God is an eternal self-sufficient, self-contained togetherness.

Novelist William Young takes an imaginative look at the Trinity in his book *The Shack*, where he portrays God as a sassy black woman, Jesus as a carpenter in a plaid shirt, and the Holy Spirit as an Asian sylph named Sarayu. Whatever its literary or theological limitations, the book effectively conveys a God who, within the Trinity, experiences loving, being loved, giving, sharing, knowing and being known, laughing, playing, and working together. You and I crave that same eternal sense of togetherness, with God and each other.

The reason humans crave relationship, companionship, friendship, and a stable, dependable, lifelong union with one other person is that we were made that way! This quality of togetherness was woven into our very being from the beginning at creation.

Collaboration

Eve was a helper for Adam, who after her arrival no longer was burdened with the entire responsibility for naming all the animals, cultivating the garden, and stewarding the earth.

My son was on the creative team that developed *Myst* and *Riven*, two very successful computer games. But the game he worked on that most intrigued me was *URU*, designed to be a 24/7 interactive communal game experience. When he was beta testing I watched as Josh, who was sitting in his office in Spokane, met a game player based in Switzerland, who asked Josh to help him mount a gondola. This had been designed into the game as a two-person task so that even the creator of the game could not accomplish it without another person's help. Given the choice, why

would a game creator design situations requiring collaborative efforts?

I think I know why. These two dramatic words in our
creation story—"Let us"—are a reminder that community,
not individuality, is at the heart of the human story. Unlike
the American Dream, based on rugged individualism, God's
dream is that we work together interdependently for the
common good. Without you and what you offer to me,
and without me and what I offer to you, and without us and
what we offer the world together, planet earth cannot
become the habitable place God created it to be. It takes a
village to steward a planet.

We are created in such a way that each of us brings
talents, perspectives, personality, heart, and mind that are
needed by others. Just as in a physical body the hands need
the fingers and the fingers need the hands, and no part of the
body can say, "I have no need of you," so we humans are
created to rely on each other. Every tribe, nation, language,
and culture offer something essential to the whole and the
whole is greater than the sum of its parts.

Becoming fully alive and fully human requires discovering God and discovering yourself, but it also involves
discovering the unique talents of others and experiencing
the release of power that happens when your gifts are pooled
with the complementary gifts of others in accomplishing
a specific mission or task. The genius of many individuals
is often overlooked, because what they offer by itself may
not seem extraordinary or even useful. Yet we all know that
one seemingly unimportant note is made richer when it is

combined with other notes to form a chord. Becoming fully human requires genuinely appreciating every person on earth and understanding that each is wondrously created in God's image. Individually and together we offer the potential to be a dazzling display of a slice of God's image.

Mother Teresa saw a glimmer of God's image in even the most emaciated, diseased, and dying pauper and poured her love and compassion onto the least of these. Were we to understand the mysteries of the universe, we would realize that the addict on the street, the Down's syndrome child, the wildly creative eccentric, and the unflappable, calm, calculating strategist each has great value and a unique contribution to make. For all of us together to make this world a habitable, civilized place, each of us must individually reach our fullest potential.

We collaborate because that is how God made us. When Jesus wanted to change the world he called twelve diverse disciples, not one superstar. Each disciple retained his individuality while being melded into a team. The apostle John was tenderhearted, Peter was impetuous and impulsively fearless, and Thomas was a cool, rational doubter. Each on his own represented wonderful possibilities and offsetting limitations, but God wove them into a rich tapestry and they became an example of what happens when God inhabits individuals and then makes them into a team.

We can't discover our distinct competence without the help of other people because sometimes they see us more clearly than we see ourselves. My friend Ralph Mattson often said that if God wanted us to see ourselves clearly, He would have put eyeballs in our fingertips. Instead our eyes look outward, so we can see others and others can see us more clearly.

Ralph's metaphor took on new meaning when I spent time with the brilliant singer-songwriter Michael Kelly Blanchard and learned how he got his start as a writer. It turns out that the young Irishman was in detention at his local high school when a teacher offered to "bail him out"—on one condition. The teacher had noticed Michael's flair for the dramatic and identified a role for him in the school play. Like any good Irishman, Blanchard figured that storytelling on stage beat being in detention, so he agreed to the conditions and the next thing he knew he was giving his premiere theatrical performance.

One day the teacher noticed Michael struggling with a page of dialogue and discovered the budding young thespian thought the portrayal of his character in that scene was inconsistent with the rest of his character's development. The teacher asked Michael to rewrite the page, and that night, because a teacher had been observant, the career of a singer-songwriter was launched. Some people are happy and some people are "happy makers." When you help another person discover their destiny as defined by their unique talents, you become both happy and a happy maker. Imagine my surprise when I learned from Michael that the teacher in the story was my friend Ralph, a man who obviously practices what he preaches.

The right collaboration brings out the best in everybody. Woody Harrelson burst on the scene in a seemingly small role in the television show *Cheers* and since that time has been a leading proponent of ensemble acting. He recently described it this way: "I love getting together and making something with a bunch of other people." After being out of the industry for a few years, a *New York Times* reporter observed, "Now Mr. Harrelson is in the midst of a rekindled affair. 'I love it,' he said of acting in films. 'I have never been a big fan of the business of motion pictures, but the process, the work, is really fun if you do it with the right people.'"[2]

It is critically important to do things with the right people. I learned this as a boy of about nine years of age when my skills as a producer emerged. My friends and I decided to put on a backyard carnival. We decided to collaborate in creating different attractions. We took a large refrigerator box, cut a paper-size hole in it, and then perched Jimmy Sellers in the box with a typewriter and set of dictionaries. Anybody could ask the box anything and it would produce an answer! We wanted a flashing light on the box so one of my friends sat in back of it plugging and unplugging the light (a low-tech, but efficient cost-effective solution!). Another kid mounted his bike and rode through the neighborhood promoting the event. My sisters worked a booth and another friend did a magic show; yet another collected the tickets. This was the first of many endeavors in which I saw the differing talents of multiple people creating something bigger than any one of us could have envisioned on our own.

It is not good for humans to be alone. Rodgers and Hammerstein, Penn and Teller, Steve Wozniak and Steven

Jobs, Paul Allen and Bill Gates, John Lennon and Paul McCartney, Marty O'Donnell and Mike Salvatori are but a few of the success stories that grew out of collaboration.

Every entrepreneurial venture I've been involved in has unfolded around wildly differing talents and personalities who started down an uncertain, unmarked road together. Many times your best friendships will be forged in the trenches with collaborators. Ray Homan and I started singing together in college back in the 1960s and now, forty years later, though we seldom sing, he's still among a handful of friends I can always count on. C. S. Lewis and J.R.R. Tolkien met with other literary types in a group they called the Inklings to read and critique each other's work. Lewis said of this company of friends, "It is only four or five people who like one another meeting to do things that they like. This is friendship. Aristotle placed it among the virtues, saying friendship causes perhaps half of all the happiness in the world."[3] Together we can spur one another toward the highest and best work we are capable of. Usually the very best happens when we join forces with others who aim for excellence and who with us shoot for the stars.

Together

In A. A. Milne's classic children's book *Now We Are Six*, one of the poems is titled *Us Two*. It tells the story of a child who can always count on Winnie the Pooh being there, no matter how alone he or she feels. "What would I do if it weren't for you?" the child asks. Pooh agrees, noting that one isn't much fun, but two can stick together.

Though we are distinct individuals, it is obvious from birth that we were created for togetherness. Yet loneliness and isolation are constant refrains in contemporary society, as evidenced by books with titles like *The Lonely Crowd* or *Bowling Alone*. A *National Geographic* headline pops out on the crowded newsstand: "Are We Alone? Searching the Heavens for Another Earth." The article declares that more than 370 planets outside of our solar system have been discovered and the Milky Way galaxy gleams with over one hundred billion stars, billions of which may possess planetary systems of their own. On many of those planets, the article continues, something like human life may exist.

Despite our justifiable fascination with life on yet-to-be discovered planets, it is the dilemma of feeling alone on our own planet that occupies most of our time and attention. Songs, poems, films, and novels tell tales of people who are isolated and alone even though they live on an overcrowded planet with billions of others. Our vocabulary is populated with words conveying the all-too-common experience: *alone, solitary, lonely, lonesome, lone, forlorn, abandoned, orphaned, desolate.* Such aloneness was never the creator's intention.

In the beginning our ancestors knew nothing of loneliness because they enjoyed intimate union with God and each other. Friendship, companionship, and deep, lasting relationships were their birthright. Our appetite for togetherness was born in Eden's garden and we carry it with us to this day. We don't know what we've lost until its gone. In a section of Mark Twain's *Eve's Diary* titled "After the Fall," Eve reminisces, "When I look back, the garden is a dream to me. It was beautiful, surpassingly beautiful, and now it is lost, and I shall not see it anymore."[4]

Lest we get ahead of our story, let's pause and reflect on the wonders of our ancestral homeland. Our universal human yearnings today are a constant reminder that there was once a time in the distant past when paradise was ours, together.

5

our ancestral homeland

Perhaps some deep-rooted atavism urges the wanderer back to lands which his ancestors left in the dim beginnings of history.

—SOMERSET MAUGHAM

Some circumstances are more conducive to being fully alive and fully human than others. Place does matter. Just ask around, "Where is the best place on earth to live?"

Hollywood producer David Geffen once said, "Move to California. Malibu is paradise." I know better, for I do, in fact, live in paradise. I live on Orcas Island, Washington, where my waking cry is, "Another day in paradise!" My claims of paradise aren't just a matter of opinion. In June

2008, Island Magazine named Orcas one of the top ten islands in the world to call home—the first not located in the Southern Hemisphere ever given that distinction—and the May 2009 issue of Forbes called Orcas "one of 10 island paradises in America."

Just reading these reports fills me with a smug pride at my good fortune at having landed in paradise. But, I must confess, we who live here know Orcas Island is not literally paradise. People get sick and die here, some are trapped in addictions, and others experience the heartache of deteriorating relationships or the trauma of financial woes. When we call Orcas paradise, what we are really saying is that it comes as close to paradise as anything we've found on earth.

At a deeper level our quest for a better or idyllic place reminds us that there is in the human heart a universal longing and collective memory for an ancestral homeland often referred to as paradise. Frederick Buechner reminds us that "the word longing comes from the same root as the word long in the sense of length in either time or space [as well as from] the word belong, so that in its full richness, to long suggests to yearn for a long time for something that is a long way off and something that we feel we belong to and that belongs to us."[1]

This proverbial paradise, where we belonged long ago and which we somehow feel belongs to us today, is described in the Bible as the Garden of Eden. Eden is a Hebrew word meaning delight and garden means an enclosed space. Eden's precise geographic location is uncertain, but it is traditionally thought to have been a lush spot in the Middle

East. Less important than its physical location is its mythic suitability for human health and happiness. Psychologists make detailed lists of universal human needs like security, sustenance, autonomy, leisure, affection, acceptance, community, meaning, and transcendence. Eden had it all!

Eden was a floral garden resplendent with the brilliant colors and enticing fragrances of the earth's botanical bounty. Eden was a vegetable garden providing food for its human inhabitants who were hungry for the succulent, organic, nutrient-rich diet that would sustain their lives. The garden was forested, providing shelter for the wild beasts. It contained meadows and open fields on which cattle could range. Like Central Park in New York City, the garden was a place for respite and recreation, with paths providing opportunities for pleasant walks for humans, who even considered such paths worthy of God. Indeed, they said (anthropomorphically), God walked through the garden one day. Eden was a secure place for both meaningful work and rest from labors and a beautiful, aesthetic location where humans could enjoy uninterrupted community with each other and God.

Contemporary artists regularly express their longing to recapture this idyllic Garden of Eden that Adam and Eve called home. The Beatles said "once there was a way to get back homeward." In the soundtrack to the movie *The Chronicles of Narnia*, musical artist Switchfoot speaks of being created for a place they'd never known, a home where they belonged. Thomas Wolfe was struck with Milton's vision in *Paradise Lost* and embedded the concept in the title of his classic work, *Look Homeward Angel*. Joni Mitchell said we are "stardust" and "golden" and we've "got to get ourselves back to the garden."

All of these refer to a place we collectively believe once existed, a place where we belonged and long for all these centuries later. Because this world is full of sorrow, heartache, disappointments, and tragedy, it is good to be reminded that we were in fact made for a different kind of world. In the Bible we learn that God originally created us for and put us in a place we could call home, where we could flourish.

The first pages of Genesis describe God blessing humans with life, liberty, and happiness. For Americans the phrase "life, liberty, and the pursuit of happiness" is reminiscent of the rights stated in our Declaration of Independence. The phrase is often said to originate with Enlightenment philosopher John Locke, but even deist Thomas Jefferson acknowledged that the Bible's creation story is the deeper, original source. Jefferson wrote, "We hold these truths to be self-evident, that all men are created equal, that they are *endowed by their creator* with certain unalienable rights, that among these are life, liberty and the pursuit of happiness."

Life

At creation God breathed life into the first humans and gave them a home in a garden teeming with life. "Let the water teem with living creatures, and let birds fly above the earth across the expanse of the sky. . . . The Lord God formed the man from the dust of the ground and breathed into his nostrils the breath of life, and the man became a living being" (Genesis 2:7).

We all agree that biological life is a precious gift. We are delighted at the birth of a puppy, a fledgling, a kitten, or a foal. Certainly anyone who has been present for the birth of a child and heard that first cry knows the surge of excitement when new life arrives on the planet. Humans began as an inanimate lump of clay until God breathed life into them, and since then, as William Blake enthuses, "everything that lives is holy, life delights in life!"

But humans do not value life simply because we are born; rather, we place value on the *way* we live our lives. From the dawn of history humans have aspired to live meaningful lives. For the Jews this meant seeking *shalom*— a complete, full, and satisfying life, a life that cannot be improved by the addition of anything more. Because the Jews understood they were created in God's image, they knew a full life required the holistic development of their unique creative, spiritual, intellectual, communicative, relational, and moral capacities.

Any aspect missing or less than it should be would result in the diminishment of *shalom*. Rabbi Jesus taught this, saying, "I am come that you might have life and have it more abundantly." Our passion for God's gift of life explains our aversion to death. Death is an enemy, the grim reaper, and a seemingly unnecessary end.

If the opposite of biological life is death, the opposite of the meaningful life is the meaningless life, and for the Jews that meant life without God. The writer of Ecclesiastes described life without God variously in different translations: "Vanity of vanities, all is vanity." "Meaningless of meaninglessness! All is meaningless!" "Futility of futilities, all is futile." "Absolutely pointless! Everything is pointless." He concluded, "The end of the matter; when all has been heard? Fear God, and keep his commandments; for that is the whole duty of everyone."

Biological life is precious, but a meaningful life is more precious. That is why Abraham Lincoln once quipped, "It's not the years in your life that count. It is the life in your years." The garden teemed with life, most notably the keepers of the garden who were aglow with the presence of God and fully human, fully alive.

Liberty

Genesis 2:16–17 says that "the Lord God commanded the man, 'You are free to eat from any tree in the garden, but you must not eat from the tree of the knowledge of good and evil, for when you eat of it you will surely die.'". If freedom is the absence of interference with the sovereignty of an individual by the use of coercion or aggression, then Adam and Eve were free. Freedom is another aspect of the image of God imprinted on us, which is why humans will always yearn for freedom; we were created to be free from the beginning.

History reveals our universal human passion for freedom. When the Jews were exiled for four hundred years in Egypt, God sent a message to Pharaoh through Moses, "Let my people go!" In America our independence was fueled by a succession of freedom lovers—pilgrims escaping religious persecution and then patriots escaping the tyranny of foreign rule. The landscape of twentieth-century Europe is dotted with active resistance to freedom-denying despots like Stalin, Hitler, and many others. Twenty years ago students protesting in China at Tiananmen Square stirred our hearts with their passion for liberation. As this is being written we are following developments in Tehran, where courageous Iranians risked death at the hands of a repressive government and a theocratic despot because they desire to be free.

Humans yearn to be free because God made us this way and we began life in an idyllic place where freedom had not yet been abused or exercised in self-destructive ways. In Buddhism paradise is Nirvana, the cessation of will. But in Judaism and Christianity paradise involves expressing our free will by exercising it for God and the good. As writer Thomas Howard is often quoted as saying: "Hell is where everyone is doing his own thing; paradise is where everyone is doing God's thing." In Eden we learned that freedom involves personal responsibility and consequences for our actions.

We are created in the image of a God who wills only good for us. The age-old question, "Is there anything God cannot do?" must be answered, "Yes! God can do anything he wills to do, but there are things his character does not allow him to do. God cannot lie, because God is truth." Mystic A. W. Tozer summarizes: "It is silly to say God can do anything, but it is scriptural to say God can do anything God wills to do."[2]

In the same way, humans were granted complete freedom except freedom to do one thing: "You are free to eat from any tree in the garden; but you must not eat from the tree of the knowledge of good and evil, for when you eat of it you will surely die." Some might say that without the knowledge of good and evil, humans were not truly free. But was not the request of the loving trustworthy creator a sufficient basis for obedience? Shall not the created ones trust the creator who has bestowed every blessing on them? Is the parent telling the child not to touch a hot stove restricting their freedom or preserving their happiness and well being?

Later, God revealed the Ten Commandments to clarify the kinds of behavior that ensure human happiness, but Adam and Eve did not need the law, nor did they need the knowledge of good and evil, for they possessed something far more powerful—the unmediated, unrestrained love of God in union with each other and God. Trusting and obeying God was their opportunity to reciprocate God's love. The secret of happiness is freedom; the secret of responsible freedom is to love and obey God and to love your neighbor as yourself.

Happiness

Humans yearn for the good and happy life because we were created for such a life. By definition, happiness is circumstantial because the word happiness means an experience related to what happens, or *happenstance*. We are happy when good things happen to us and unhappy when bad circumstances are inflicted upon us.

Psychologist Abraham Maslow studied the human quest for happiness and found it involved progressing through five different levels of fulfillment beginning with our most basic physiological needs: breathing, water, sleep, food, clothing, and shelter. At Level 2 we seek to meet our safety needs: health, personal, financial. Level 3 refers to meeting our social needs for friendship, intimacy, and a supportive and communicative family. At Level 4 we meet our needs for self-esteem and being valued by others. For Maslow the highest level was self-actualization, the point in life where we have fully developed our moral, creative, and intelligence capacities.

In Eden God created the ideal conditions for our happiness, the ideal circumstances in which to fulfill Maslow's paradigm. Basic necessities were provided for; Eden was completely safe and there was no death. Social needs were met through a spouse and the promise of children to come of their sexual union. Humans were held in the highest esteem by God, who made them just a little lower than the angels and gave them dominion over all the earth. In Eden the first humans were morally pure and innocent. They were given meaningful work, purposeful activity that was both mental and physical. In Eden there was no workaholism because God set a rhythmic pattern of rest and leisure. In Eden humans enjoyed intimate fellowship with their creator. They were placed in a lush garden on a glorious planet with a silvery moon, a bright warm sun, billions of stars, fresh flowing rivers, deep vast oceans, and towering mountains. In the beginning human life was purposeful with outlets for our creative, spiritual, intellectual, communicative, relational, and moral capacities.

But as we now know, the gifts of life, liberty, and happiness found in Eden were contingent on innocent humans loving and trusting the creator, and sadly we also know that our ancestral paradise was lost due to our ancestors' rebellion. Since that time there has been within each human a deep sense that we are not fully at home in the world as it is.

Somerset Maugham captured this tension perfectly:

> I have an idea that some men are born out of their
> due place. Accident has cast them amid certain sur-
> roundings, but they have always a nostalgia for a
> home they know not. They are strangers at their
> birthplace, and the leafy lanes they have known from
> childhood or the populous streets in which they
> have played, remain but a place of passage. They may
> spend their whole lives aliens among their kindred
> and remain aloof among the only scenes they have
> ever known. Perhaps it is this sense of strangeness
> that sends men far and wide in the search for
> something permanent, to which they may attach

themselves. Perhaps some deep-rooted atavism urges the wanderer back to lands which his ancestors left in the dim beginnings of history.[3]

Our collective memories of a place called home haunt us, because we are so acutely aware that we do not live there now. In *The Wizard of Oz* when Dorothy is transported to the beauty and splendor of Oz, she utters the famous lines, "Toto, I have a feeling we're not in Kansas anymore." Our experience is the opposite. We awaken each day aware that our paradise has been lost. Where are we? What happened? Can we ever get back to the garden?

III

the human problem

*our devastating
diminishment and
dehumanization*

6

fallen, broken, and sick unto death

God does not die on the day when we cease to believe in a personal deity, but we die on the day when our lives cease to be illuminated by the steady radiance, renewed daily, of a wonder, the source of which is beyond all reason.

—DAG HAMMERSKJOLD

My great-grandfather left what is now called the Gold Coast of Lake Zurich in Switzerland to attend seminary and then to pastor a small German-speaking church in North Dakota. I've visited his hometown in Herrliberg, Switzerland, and I've seen the badlands of North Dakota. I mean no disrespect to the Dakotas, but having seen both it is hard to say from a human standpoint that he "traded up." I imagine my grandfather going to bed one night in a lovely chalet in the lush farmlands of Herrliberg with its lakefront vistas and picturesque snowcapped mountains in the distance and then waking up the next morning in the barren Badlands of North Dakota the next, and asking, "What happened?"

This is our situation today. In the beginning our ancestors were created in God's image and placed in a delightful place ideally suited to meet their every need, a place where they could be fully human and fully alive. Yet you and I were not born in such a time and place and do not live there now. What happened? How did we leave our ancestral homeland for what is by comparison a badland? This chapter in our sad tale can be broadly referred to as our *dehumanization*—the shattering and deterioration of everything that made us special.

The Fall

One metaphorical way to think of our human saga is as a skydiving adventure that ends badly. There are sports like skydiving where the fun is in the fall. Friends tell me the thrill is in the speed and the exhilarating rush of death-defying unrestrained freedom. They say the air gently cushions and holds you up so you don't even realize you are plummeting to earth. Perhaps in their initial bite into the forbidden fruit, our ancestors felt the adrenaline surge as they hurtled toward the wicked wild unknown.

But there are falls that go desperately wrong. On rare occasions the parachute does not open. You pull the cord and it does not respond. More often fatalities occur when the skydiver waits too long to release the parachute, or tries a risky landing, or crashes into power lines or trees. In every case, when things go badly wrong, there comes that split second when you realize the situation is beyond your control and you are headed for disaster. This is the moment when the thrill of falling is exchanged for the irrevocable pain and brokenness of all who have fallen.

You and I are descended from a long line of spiritual skydivers. Our fall began with Adam and Eve, who fell from an idyllic life to expulsion from Eden. Their fall is the most well-known and consequential in history. The mythic outline is all too familiar: a serpent seeking to do them harm, half-truths seducing them into rebellion, and the first displacement of the higher force above through a defiant declaration of human autonomy. With Adam and Eve's defiant act, for the first moment since the dawning of time someone other than God was the center of human existence. Angels quaked and the planet groaned as the human revolt deteriorated in quick succession to hiding from God, the blame game, and the first murder. Adam and Eve's rebellion and subsequent fall was the precursor of our own, and their outcome foretold ours—when you fall, something gets broken. In an instant we were transformed from fully human to fallen, broken humans.

An artist friend of mine was asked to do an installation for an ancient cathedral in England. He sculpted papier-mâché into what appeared to be broken clay pots and filled the aisles with them. The broken pots streamed toward the Eucharist table at the front of the cathedral. This symbol of broken pots reminds us that we were made to be whole but after the fall are but broken pots, parts of us are missing and we are less than we were intended to be. Until we know we are broken we cannot be repaired; until we know we have fallen and lay shattered on the ground we cannot be put back together again.

Sadly, Adam and Eve's moment of folly was not the last, for every human since has been a spiritual skydiver, carving out our own personal, unique path to human enthronement and estrangement from God. Since the fateful events in the garden, every human has shown symptoms of a second metaphor for the human condition, what Søren Kierkegaard called a sickness unto death. This sickness is the source of our communal sense of angst, loss, and longing. The story of Adam and Eve's fall and expulsion from the garden explains the intuitive universal feeling that we've got to get ourselves back to the garden.

A Sickness unto Death

Since ours is a sickness unto death, it is critically important that our human illness be properly diagnosed and treated, or our quest for a full and complete human life will never be successful.

To illustrate, let me tell you a personal story that happened when I played college basketball. For those of you who have met me, you'll have to take this next part on faith. In college I was a tall, skinny, undersized forward whose coaches constantly tried to help me gain weight. Some people say my rebounding prowess was extraordinary, but I also possessed an uncanny ability to miss free throws under pressure, or truthfully, even without pressure. When I got playing time I spent most of it fighting it out for rebounds under the backboards. In one particularly brutal battle I took a sharp-edged elbow under my eye. My tender skin split open and the blood flowed from the fresh wound like water from Niagara Falls. Nothing could stop this mighty torrent so I was driven off to a local emergency room for treatment.

In each life one can point to memorable experiences, and what happened next is among mine.

The doctor entered the room, took one look at me, and asked, "Which finger is it?" Somehow he had been told I had a broken finger and despite the blood draining from my face he was dead set on treating my finger.

The moral of the story for me is simple: proper treatment begins with the right diagnosis. I've since learned that what is true in the physical realm is also true in the spiritual realm. Unless we accurately assess our situation we will never identify the right and adequate spiritual treatment.

For just a moment I'd like you to think of me as your doctor who, after running the tests and diagnosing your health, is bringing you a complete report. The news about you is not good. I ask you to take a seat and I begin by placing your situation in a broader context.

I carefully explain the situation to you. There is a highly contagious illness sweeping through the human race. It has been passed from generation to generation. It is a pandemic, a global epidemic that has spread internationally with unprecedented speed to every country and village on the earth. The illness is terminal. It is a sickness unto death. One hundred percent of the people who get it die.

This disease is similar to leprosy, but worse. Leprosy eats away at the flesh, but this systemic disease is even more sinister, because in addition to eventually causing your physical death, the polluting, corrosive effect of this disease will slowly eat away at every dimension of your existence, diminishing you beyond recognition. J.R.R. Tolkien captured the image of this wasting away and dehumanization in the character of Gollum, the emaciated shell of what was once a vibrant human.

This disease pollutes the way you think. It disrupts your relationships. It causes you to do hurtful and harmful things even when you know they are wrong. It affects your spirit, causing you to feel defeated. It diminishes your creativity. This is unquestionably and undeniably the most devastating illness ever to infect the human race.

Now I tell you the worst news of all: *you have this disease.*

Before you panic, let me offer some comfort. I can empathize with you because I am also afflicted with this sickness unto death. I'm something of an expert on this disease, having spent most of my life trying to understand its symptoms, causes, and cures. Let me share some of what I've learned.

The Symptoms

My parents informed me about this disease when I was a child. They explained that ever since Adam and Eve's rebellion in the garden, all humans have followed in their footsteps and as a result have experienced a systemic unraveling of their relationship with God, with each other, and with the earth itself. To dehumanize means to deprive of human qualities or attributes. The fall and our sickness unto death tarnish God's image in our lives, diminishing us in every way—spiritually, intellectually, creatively, relationally, and morally.

It wasn't until I was in college in the San Francisco Bay Area in the 1960s that I recognized the symptoms of this disease all around me, because although the sixties were about sex, drugs, and rock 'n' roll, they were also a time for honest self-examination and spiritual quest. The sense of loss and diminishment was widespread. We read Camus, Sartre, and other angst-ridden existentialists. Our music took on prophetic overtones, exposing the symptoms of our discontent. Joni Mitchell, Paul Simon, Bob Dylan, and many others expressed the heart cry of a troubled generation: we wanted to be more, we needed to be more, we felt we should be more than we were both individually and as a society.

Film, art, and music exposed the fault lines of familial unhappiness and the hypocrisy of cold, unhappy marriages endured for the sake of the kids. Sons were alienated from fathers, mothers from daughters, and the façade of 1950s familial bliss erupted into open hostility. Divorce rates skyrocketed. Two World Wars and a Great Depression had birthed a quest for financial stability, and rampant material-ism ate at our souls. Credit cards, bigger homes complete with private swimming pools, were masking a subterranean volcano of unease that was about to explode. In wildness is the preservation of the earth and our stewardship of the planet was called into question; we were paving paradise and destroying it in the process. Deeper still was the nag-ging sense of personal aloneness and isolation. To quote Paul Simon: I am a rock, I am an island, and a rock feels no pain. It doesn't weep. The failed attempt at cultural transformation in the 1960s and the ongoing march of mean-inglessness has given rise to our nouveau nihilism today.

The Band-Aids

Students of history know ours is only the most recent generation to feel a sense of despair about our situation. Centuries ago the writer of Ecclesiastes told the story of a man who had reached the conclusion that all was mean-ingless. He described his many failed attempts at finding a purposeful life: women, wine, and wealth. We see the same futile pursuits today.

Today we see contemporary versions of treating serious illness with insufficient remedies. "All you need is love" is an inadequate prescription for a distrustful generation whose problem chiefly consists of an inability to love. Romance seems an odd solution for a generation increasingly skep-tical of marriage and wary of lifelong commitment. Our sexual liberation reduced acts of personal intimacy as the expression of the deepest love, affection, and commitment to animalistic responses to merely physical drives. Our partying and playing were simply contemporary forms of the ancient diversions—wine, women, and song. We have elevated sensate amusements to their most exalted place in human history, spending thousands of hours watching TV or films, playing games, or listening to more music, but enjoying it less. Drugs, whether pharmaceutical or cinematic, audio or visual, provide a temporary respite or worse, are physical, spiritual, and intellectual destroyers.

The distinction between education and wisdom has become embarrassingly obvious as generations of the brightest and the best know all too well that you can attain all the academic degrees in the world and still retain the baseness of selfishness, wrong acts, and a fallen nature. As one of my professors said, in our society it is possible to have a lot of degrees and no temperature! Education without wisdom is folly.

We were told that greed is good, but the wealthiest nation in the history of the world is also the most anxious, unhappy, and overmedicated. Seventy percent of our economy is made up of consumer spending and we retain storage units to contain the overflow of our stuff. Yet our materially full lives have not sated our spiritual appetites.

Years of human experience have taught us that we will transmit our pain if we don't transform and resolve it, but try as we may, the pain lingers and the hurting continues. In our therapeutic age we've given ourselves permission to obsess about our own personal emotional needs, but the

pain does not lift and we understand what novelist Saul
Bellow quipped, "Socrates said, 'The unexamined life is not
worth living'; my paraphrase is, 'The examined life makes
you wish you were dead.'"[1]

Our thoughts, our art, our values, our moral deci-
sions, our relationships all betray our fallenness and sickness,
and yet having failed to address our universal sickness unto
death adequately, we slip into denial about our human
condition. The burgeoning self-help movement feeds this
self-delusion. As the old George Carlin joke goes, "I went
to a bookstore and asked the saleswoman, 'Where's the self-
help section?' She said if she told me, it would defeat the
purpose."[2] Because rugged self-determinism is the essence
of the American mythology, self-help has blossomed into a
billion-dollar industry that exploits our sickness unto death
but cannot heal it.

Until we know we are sick we cannot be healed, and
all these attempted cures address the symptoms of our sickness unto death but not the root cause. They all assume there
is a self-administered cure for our own illness, but our sickness unto death is rooted in something too deep for home
remedies and self-treatment.

So if you want to cure your soul sickness where do
you start? What is the root cause of our sickness unto death?

As a young man Aleksandr Solzhenitsyn hoped the
Russian Revolution would right all wrongs, but after endur-
ing ten years in the gulag, all pretense was stripped away and
he became a realist who explored the older truths. Wanting
to find a cure for the human condition he spent the rest of

his life searching for the root causes of the human situation. After years of reflection, near the end of his life he reached his conclusion.

> Over a half century ago, while I was still a child,
> I recall hearing a number of old people offer the
> following explanation for the great disasters that had
> befallen Russia: "Men have forgotten God; that's why
> all this has happened." Since then I have spend
> well-nigh 50 years working on the history of our
> revolution; in the process I have read hundreds of
> books, collected hundreds of personal testimonies,
> and have already contributed eight volumes of my
> own toward the effort of clearing away the rubble
> left by that upheaval. But if I were asked today to
> formulate as concisely as possible the main cause of
> the ruinous revolution that swallowed up some 60
> million of our people, I could not put it more accu-
> rately than to repeat: "Men have forgotten God; that's
> why all this has happened."[3]

If our rebellion against God and our departure from an intimate relationship with God were the beginning of our dehumanization and unraveling, does it not stand to reason that the restoration of our relationship with God would be the most likely way to restore our essential humanness?

The Root Cause

Just as diseases that kill the body have names, the sickness of the soul has a name, one that has been acknowledged in previous generations but less so today. The cause of our soul sickness is summarized in a three-letter word: sin, which simply means to miss the mark or fall short.

Remember when you first held a bow and arrow in your hand? You pulled back with all your might and the arrow fell limply in front of you, far short of the intended mark. Remember how you worked at propelling the arrow farther forward and finally got the distance but lacked accuracy? The arrow flew wildly to the left or right of center. These images help us understand the meaning of the word sin, which in both Hebrew and Greek means to miss the mark, or to fall short of the mark. Sin is more than the violation of a moral code. The essence of sin is to fall short of who we were created to be. We were created for an intimate union with God and each other, we were made to be whole and to be a stunning reflection of God's image, but we have missed the mark and are less than God created us to be. Any attitude or behavior that makes us less human, less than who God made us to be, is sin.

You may think sin is primarily about the bad things you do or have done, but that is not so; sin is first and foremost a relational disruption that begins with a declaration of autonomy from God. Immediately after Adam and Eve rebelled against God, God asked, "Where are you?" God knew Adam had abandoned the union he had enjoyed with God. Adam was no longer without guile or shame and was suddenly uncomfortable in God's presence. The union with God for which Adam and Eve were created was shattered.

Furthermore, Adam and Eve's allegiance to God and promise to love, obey, and serve God were violated. As Bob

Dylan reminds us, everybody's got to serve somebody. He narrowed it down to two choices: you are either serving devil or you are serving the Lord. The problem with Adam and Eve is not the act of eating the fruit but rather it is that they did not trust and obey God the Father when he commanded them not to do so. When they ate the fruit what they were really doing was pledging their allegiance to themselves and the serpent instead of where it belonged, with God who created and loved them.

When we abandon our allegiance to God we lose intimacy with God, violating the essence of who we are. We are dehumanized in the process. Swedish diplomat Dag Hammerskjold put it this way, "God does not die on the day when we cease to believe in a personal deity, but we die on the day when our lives cease to be illuminated by the steady radiance, renewed daily, of a wonder, the source of which is beyond all reason."[4]

So sin is first and foremost the betrayal of a love relationship with our creator, and it happens every time we displace our allegiance to God with allegiance to ourselves or to other gods. There is no middle ground, for as Rabbi Abraham Heschel succinctly says, "God is of no importance unless He is of Supreme importance." The psalmist understood this and cried out, "Who have I in heaven but God and there is none on earth that I desire beside you" (Psalm 73:25).

The further we drift from God the more prone we are to behaviors that diminish our humanness. God revealed the Ten Commandments not to ruin our fun, but to protect us from dehumanizing behaviors.

Worshipping other gods diminishes us. Disregarding a Sabbath rest will result in our physical or emotional weariness. Dishonoring parents violates our first and primary relationship. Murder, adultery, stealing all make us less human. Ben Franklin recognized the dehumanizing effects of sin when he said, "Sin is not hurtful because it is forbidden; it is forbidden because it is hurtful."

Why would we engage in behaviors that diminish us? The Talmud, which contains rabbinic reflections on Jewish law and ethics, offers an important clue, "Sin is sweet in the beginning but bitter in the end." There is an initial flush of exhilaration in enthroning self in place of God, in the sensuous adulterous act, in seizing what we want that is not ours, but eventually most of us learn the hard way that we are punished *by our sins,* not just for our sins, and that the short-term pleasures of sinful behaviors bear long-term painful consequences.

Yet once we have headed down the wrong road we find ourselves irrepressibly drawn to self-destructive behavior. The devastating truth is that sin, like any physical disease, takes on a life of its own, one over which we have limited control. When we shift our allegiance from God to our self and begin behaving in dehumanizing ways, the external power of sin becomes internalized. Once sin is internalized it metastasizes like a tumor, and then begins to spread through your whole life.

Another metaphor for sin is found in the term "bent-ness." Back to the archery analogy: if the arrow is bent you will not be to hit the mark no matter how you try.

The apostle Peter said, "A man is a slave to whatever has mastered him." Our attempts at "becoming better people" fail because we are bent and can no longer hit the mark; we cannot hit the target no matter how hard we try. The apostle Paul said, "In my sinful nature, I am a slave to sin" and "The sinful mind is hostile to God. It does not submit to God's law, nor can it do so."

We are broken, we are sick unto death, and we are bent and unable to hit the target, all of us falling short and missing the mark. Yet, tragically, among the side effects of our dehumanizing disease are memory loss, drowsiness, and a euphoric sense of wellness even as we waste away in our illness. Wilco's Jeff Tweedy wrote the song *Hell Is Chrome* after going through drug rehab. In the song he describes how seductively attractive drugs were in his life. He was lulled into complacency and felt no fear because in his words, the devil deceived him into feeling like he was wel- comed and made him feel like he belonged. The devil did not appear in an easily identifiable red suit and horns; the devil disguised himself as a trustworthy friend. Like Adam and Eve and every human since, Tweedy was deceived and paid the price.

How do you warn people of danger when they feel safe? How do you awaken a person who doesn't know he is asleep? How do you heal a person who thinks she is well? How do you reason with the irrational? How do you elevate truth and beauty in an age when the ugly is thought to be beautiful and the beautiful is considered irrelevant and passé? How do you learn to love deeply in an age of superficiality, sensual distortion, and unfettered lust? How do you become fully human when fallen humans have become the accepted norm?

And so today we've left the safety of an intimate union with God in Eden for the wildness of the Badlands. It is as if we are alone in a hostile land.

7

alone in a hostile land

Everything's supposed to be different than what it is.

—DANNY GLOVER IN *GRAND CANYON*

The effects of our fall and sickness unto death are societal, not just personal. When individuals are sick unto death the culture they create reveals the symptoms of that illness and puts them on display. When you watch the news, every tragic story involving substandard, dehumanized behaviors is a poignant reminder of the ongoing impact of the fall's effects.

We can be lulled into complacency, thinking that inhuman behaviors are normal, but occasionally we see things more clearly. After the horrors of war C. S. Lewis saw our fallen human condition and the evil influences of the serpent all around him. He wrote these lines, "Enemy-occupied territory—that is what the world is."[1] The prophet Isaiah had a stunning vision of God, and when he saw the stark contrast between God's bright purity and the darkness and pollution of humans he cried, "I am a man of unclean lips and I dwell amongst a people of unclean lips."

In the film *Grand Canyon* Danny Glover, playing the role of tow-truck driver Simon, summarizes the human dilemma in his message to a young gang leader. Mack (an attorney played by Kevin Kline) is on his way home from a Lakers' game when he takes a wrong exit, gets lost, and ends up with car trouble in a bad part of town. He calls a tow truck, but before it arrives a local gang moves slowly and menacingly toward his car. Just in time, Simon arrives to intervene. He takes the leader of the gang aside and tells him the world isn't supposed to work this way. He's supposed to be able to do his job without asking the gang for permission. Kline is supposed to be able to wait in his car without getting attacked. Simon ends the conversation with the classic line, "Everything's supposed to be different than what it is."

Everything is supposed to be different than what it is—what a perfect way to describe the contrast between the way God intended life to be and the devastatingly diminished life we live on earth now.

We feel alone because we are alienated from God, our self, each other, and the earth itself. Created for intimacy with God and once at ease and fulfilled in God's presence, humans are now filled with dread in God's presence, like the character in C. S. Lewis's *Great Divorce* who encounters a heavenly man: "Here was an enthroned and shining, god, whose ageless spirit weighed upon mine like a burden of solid gold."[2]

We are alienated from our self, unable to see ourselves clearly, unable to unearth and face down our own degradation and fallenness. We know the dark night of the soul. We seek a pure heart because we are all too aware of the pollution residing in our heart and mind. We know what it means to not be at home with ourselves, to fear what is hidden, to try to hide who we are from others, to feel shame, need, lust, helplessness, to feel hopeless, to want too much, to feel continually empty and sorrowful.

We want to be vulnerable and honest, to know at least one other person and be known, but try as we might not one human is able to completely break through to another, there is always a reserve, an unopened file or a clever mask. We can't seem to avoid conflict and alienation. Wars and rumors of wars have been our lot since Cain killed Abel. We are instruments of division instead of instruments of peace. The things we want to do are the things we cannot do and the things we don't want to do are the things that we do.

We are separated from the earth itself. We've lost our connection to the land, to fresh soil, pure water, and unpolluted air. The sanctity of the plants and animals we were commissioned to care for has been diminished. We are takers not givers, users not producers, pillagers not stewards. If our call is to leave the planet in better shape than we found it, generation after generation have failed in this most basic trust. Philosopher Charles Handy calls ours the "Age of the Hungry Spirit," a spiritually impoverished age. Our individual diminishment, our alienation from God, self, each other, and the earth itself, has resulted in a cultural diminishment, for only a well soul can produce a healthy culture. So we produce the only culture we are capable of creating—a shallow, superficial, mindless celebrity culture, sustained not by ideas or craft but by money, marketing, and technology. We've substituted lies for the truth, ugliness for beauty, and evil for good. We are adrift.

T. S. Eliot said, "No culture has appeared or developed except together with a religion: according to the point of view of the observer, the culture will appear to be the product of the religion, or the religion the product of the culture."[3] Sadly, today's Christian subculture is often a mirror image of the broader culture, offering a "Christianity-Lite" version of a shallow celebrity culture and building a parallel universe, a subculture of imitative entertainment. Whether the hungry soul turns to culture or religion, it does not find the nourishment it needs.

The metaphors Jesus used two thousand years ago are even more apt today. We are lost like sheep without a shepherd. We love darkness more than light. We are shallow soil, incapable of receiving the seed of the good news. We have built our house upon sand instead of rock. We have sought an earthly kingdom first, loving money, the latest fashion, and bigger and more extravagant homes. We've abandoned the simplicity of God's kingdom for the temporary pleasures of this earth. We've pursued our upward earthly mobility at the expense of spiritual health, vitality, and growth. We've acquired more "stuff" while ignoring the poor and destitute.

God warned that no aspect of human life would be left untouched by the fall and every aspect of our lives is being diminished by the fall—our relationships with each other, with the earth, with our work, and with God. Our great unraveling and dehumanizing decline began with Adam and Eve's rebellion and has been picking up steam ever since.

We've complacently accepted the lesser life as our only option. Once after a lecture in which I spoke about our dehumanized age a college student complained about my comments, saying, "I love my culture." As we talked it became apparent that her issue was not with my critique. She agreed that our popular culture is generally superficial and mindless—she just didn't think it was a problem!

Where previous generations were often dehumanizing in barbaric, brutal, and obvious ways, our dehumanization has been subtler; it's slow but sure, like the proverbial frog that boils to death in water that slowly comes to a boil. Virtually every dominant force in our contemporary culture threatens human existence, but having marinated in this stew for a few decades many people are quite comfortable with things the way they are. In our dehumanized condition we have forgotten what fully alive and fully human looks like.

To Be Human Again—at a Glance

My mother suffered from dementia, and as her condition progressed she was often unable to recognize even her closest friends and family. When Ronald Reagan slipped into this condition, his wife Nancy said the disease was the equivalent of a long good-bye. I think in the twenty-first century, many people have forgotten what fully alive and truly human looks like. We're caught in the long good-bye and we live in a culture that has accepted its fallen condition and has said a definitive farewell to the truly human life.

But not everyone is satisfied with the status quo. Because you have read this far, I suspect you are among those who desire to be fully human and fully alive, but you are dwelling in a land that is hostile to your quest for rehumanization. For those with eyes to see, virtually every aspect of life around you is at odds with the way things are supposed to be. What might a fully human life look like?

To Be Fully Human Means to Seek
God and Nurture Your Soul

For those seeking to be fully human, cultivating the spiritual life will come first in an age when daily preoccupations are with what we will eat, what we will wear, and where we will live. John de Graaf produced a PBS series called *Affluenza*, which he defined as a painful, contagious, socially transmitted condition of overload, debt, anxiety, and waste resulting from the dogged pursuit of more. He listed some of the symptoms: shopping fever (mall mania), credit card debt, bankruptcies, greed and envy, homes congested with stuff, a shortage of time, declining savings, an overload of possessions, an ache for meaning, families in which money is used to express love, marriages in which arguments focus on money, the general feeling that there is never enough. People who suffer from this disease end up working to make a dying, not a living, because no matter how much they work and earn they are never satisfied and always need more—their spirit dies a slow painful death. Resisting the spirit of the age will require bulletproofing our lives and spirits against affluenza and acquisitiveness. It will also require shifting our attention away from the temporal to the spiritual, from satisfying the sensate to nurturing the soul. Jesus said that if we seek God's kingdom first, our daily needs like food, clothing, and shelter will be taken care of. Being fully human means becoming one of the God-smitten, whose spiritual life is more real than the physical and for whom this life is but a prelude to the next.

To Be Fully Human Means to Cultivate Your Mind

I recently was seated on a plane next to a stranger named Michael, who had a Ph.D. in history and a doctorate from Harvard Law School. He was a highly educated, intelligent, and questing spirit. Our conversation ranged from spiritual journey (he was raised Jewish but has spent considerable time seeking enlightenment in the Himalayas) to the "dumbing down" of American cultural life. We both decried the deterioration of the media into what researcher Deborah Tannen describes as "an argument culture," one that uses controversial topics for entertainment value, working the extremes instead of seeking common ground through rational dialogue.

Then Michael used a term I hadn't heard in ages and the light went on. "America," he said, "lacks a middle-brow culture." Fleshing out the idea of "middlebrow," he described highbrow culture as elitist and academic and lowbrow culture as diversionary and vacuous, adding, "America once had a thriving middlebrow culture." In his definition, "middlebrow individuals" are interested in thinking through ideas and issues, but are turned off equally by both highbrow pretensions and lowbrow mind-lessness. Middlebrow culture is where academics and mere mortals once met to converse; it is where we forged a path that shunned academic theory without application and rejected the dumbing down of culture. Anglican theologian, literary critic, and novelist Harry Blamires reminds us that this issue is of particular concern among Jesus' followers: "If Christians cannot communicate as thinking beings, they are reduced to encountering one another only at the shallow level of gossip and small talk. Hence the perhaps peculiarly modern problem—the loneliness of the thinking Christian."[4]

To Be Fully Human Means Creativity and Excellence in All You Do

Producing quality work by honing your craft and becoming skillful is critical in an age that favors the "mass-produced, low-cost, young, sexy, witty, transient, glamorous, gimmicky, expendable, and popular." In a superficial, "marketized" age, commitment to craft requires a countercultural pilgrimage. Shouldn't people made by God be blazing creative new artistic trails? Shouldn't they create good, true, and beautiful work, work that calls forth our best talent, uses the finest materials, and aims at pleasing God but carries the delightful added benefit of bringing joy to other humans? C. S. Lewis and J.R.R. Tolkien stand as examples of men whose well-crafted work has stood the test of time. They were old-school followers of Jesus who saw the relationship between the artistic, intellectual quality of their work and the depth of their devotion to God. Though excellence is not demanded or expected by our culture, it is the aim produced by an internal fire lit within those in whom God's image is shining forth. Whatever we do with our talents we should say at the end of each day, "It is good."

To Be Fully Human Means Developing In-Person Relationships in a Virtual Age

In this technologically wired culture many humans are substituting a frenzied shallow connectivity for more demanding and rewarding deep personal relationships with a few people. Twitter, texting, Facebook, and other kinds of virtual relationships and communities are no substitute for in-person relationships that go deep. What Marshall McLuhan warned us of has come true. Electronic devices have been seamlessly and deeply connected to the human central nervous system and the devices are now controlling and managing us, working us over completely. When harnessed by humans, technology is useful, but when technology wields a controlling or compulsive force in human life, we are dehumanized in the process. This is happening today and to resist is countercultural but essential if humans are to retain our essential humanness.

Personal relationships are at the core of humanness and while electronics can be an aid for relationships forged in person, they are a poor substitute. God placed our persons in bodies and disembodied contact is not the same as a personal relationship. As a talk-show host I communicated with thousands of people who came to know me at a certain level and I came to know and appreciate them. Readers know authors in this way. But a deep authentic relationship involves life in person and in physical community.

Though Jesus came to reach the whole world, he did so relationally. God did not choose to send Jesus in a digital age, but in a highly relational one. Jesus focused on direct human contact with relatively few people and by example showed that small is beautiful. When he came to earth he focused on an out-of-the-way, seemingly inconsequential place and invested his life deeply in twelve people, three of whom received even more of his time. He communicated with the masses and fed five thousand, but for the most part concentrated on a few relationships that could go much deeper.

To Be Fully Human Means Learning to Love, Forgive, and Accept Each Other

In an age of self-love, the love of many has grown cold. The three powerful words "I love you" have been cheapened by their casual use and their verbal expression without verifying practical acts in daily life. To love is to sacrifice, modify, adjust, or compromise our desires and interests for those of another. To love is primarily an action verb, not a noun or adjective. Goodness starts with you and your heart. Goodness flows from a good heart into your relationships, starting with those who you see each day, your family. Until the frightened self transcends fear and risks love, the warmth and cheer you have to give will not be added to the available stock of kindness and mercy the world needs. Our age is ravaged by all manner of abusive relationships, and children and adults alike bear the scars of emotional, physical, sexual, or verbal battering. Wounds, bitterness, and enmity are passed from one generation to the next. If you pursue a fully human life you will break the cycle by extending love and forgiveness to those who hurt you. We are those who will replace anger, rejection, and revenge with love.

To Be Fully Human Means to Embrace Moral
and Intellectual Certitude in a Relativistic Age

Human civilization depends on moral standards and reason
codified into laws. Today relativism pervades every area of
life—morally, ethically, relationally, and intellectually—and
it is producing tragic results in our individual lives and in
society.

A few years ago that great theological tome the *Wall
Street Journal* put it this way. "The U.S. has a drug problem
and a high school sex problem and a welfare problem and
an AIDS problem and a rape problem. None of this will
go away until more people in positions of responsibility
are willing to come forward and explain, in frankly moral
terms, that some of the things people do nowadays are
wrong."[5] Thus, even a financial journal recognizes that our
nation's financial crisis is no more serious than our moral
crisis and that the two are related.

The apostle John said Jesus revealed the glory of God
because Jesus was full of grace and truth (John 1:14). As
my friend Nigel says, grace without truth is romanticism,
truth without grace is legalism, and where grace and truth
are fully expressed there is dynamism.

To Be Fully Human Means to Rediscover
the Proper Rhythm of Human Life

On the seventh day God rested and later God commanded
humans to set aside a day of rest. In so doing, God identified rest and the proper pacing in life as essentially human.

There is a story of a Western traveler in Africa who hired locals to guide him on a jungle trek to a distant village. In the late afternoon the guides stopped to set up camp for the night. The Westerner, eager to arrive at his destination, vigorously protested, arguing that by pushing ahead they could make their destination by nightfall. "No," said the guide. "We will stop here to allow our souls to catch up with our bodies."

If ever there was an age when souls need to catch up with bodies it is this one. The rhythm of the seven-day week with one day of rest, the four seasons with their variations of pace and tone—these are gifts from God, reminders of the need for unhurried rhythm and balance in our personal and professional lives. Centeredness and grounding, a balanced life, these are marks of the fully alive, fully human soul. Anything less harms you and those around you. The tyranny of the urgent in an age of overcommitment reminds us that nothing is more important than knowing what should be given place and space, of what is included and what, therefore, is excluded.

To Be Fully Human Means to See the Image of God, Value, and Worth in Everyone You Meet

As a child I watched my literate, culturally refined father sit on the bumper of a logging truck laughing and joking with a rough-hewn, foul-mouthed logger. When I was four my dad brought home two Chinese workers he had met at the docks when their freighter was offloading its cargo.

Dad wanted to practice his Chinese and hear firsthand news from the faraway land. I learned by my father's example that each person has worth and that we can celebrate our differences rather than fear them.

When I was nineteen I spent three months in Indonesia, first on the island of Java, which is Muslim, and then on Bali, which is Hindu, and finally on Kalimantan, which is animist. Since then, in my travels to over fifty countries, I've discovered in each one threads of common humanness woven into the fabric of personal and cultural life. Our divisions are largely based on fear of the unknown and misunderstandings about the known. We divide people by age, race, religion, ethnicity, nationality, gender, income, education, and in dozens of other ways. But once you understand that a loving God crafted each human with unique value and worth, it becomes easier to see those qualities in everyone you meet, regardless of cultural differences.

A Whole Person

In sum, being fully human means becoming a whole person—in body, mind, spirit, creativity, relationships, and morality—despite living in a compartmentalized, fragmented age.

During the Renaissance the aim of education was to integrate the disciplines, but today the academic world is built around separate disciplines, disconnected and siloed from the others. In such a climate the specialist has replaced the generalist. Becoming an expert in your area of distinct competence is good, but limiting your development to just one thing makes you a lesser person than you were created to be. Each of us has been designed by God so that there are certain subjects and pursuits that you are naturally drawn to and suited for, but you have also been created with a range of capacities that should not be allowed to atrophy by disuse. The athlete can be a reader, the reader can jog, the loner can emerge from solace to enjoy a glass of wine with a friend, the gregarious can withdraw to solitude, the scientist can play the piano, and the pianist can grow plants. The key is to discover who you are in your completeness and then cultivate every aspect of who you are to become the fullest expression of who God made you to be.

Everything is supposed to be different than what it is. Once you see the contrast between what is and what could and should be, you are ready to begin your pilgrimage back to being fully alive and fully human. But choosing live a fully human life in the land of fallen humans means you will be, in the words of the apostle Peter, "an alien and stranger in the world" (1 Peter 2:11). Your new life will be decidedly countercultural and if you dedicate yourself to such a life, you will come face-to-face with the truth that you are unable to achieve this new fully human life on your own.

Jesus told the story of a prodigal son who reached the place where he could no longer tolerate the dissonance between the way things could and should be and life as he was actually experiencing it.

Coming to his senses was the first step back to a fuller, more satisfying life. The fully alive, fully human life is available to anyone who, like the prodigal son, comes to his or her senses.

IV

your path to fully human

*the way to fully alive
and fully human*

8

coming to
your senses

When he came to his senses, he said:
"I will arise and go back to my father."
—PARABLE OF THE PRODIGAL SON

How do you know that you are not now asleep and dreaming? It is a question I first encountered in my freshman Philosophy 101 class. Deceptively simple yet deliciously complex, answering the question required us to plumb the depths of our numb little minds for an understanding of knowing, awareness, consciousness, and essential humanness.

When it comes to the spiritual essence that is the basis for our fullest humanness there is ample evidence that most humans *are* asleep and dreaming. It is no accident that the spiritual masters describe humans variously as asleep, or blind, or born physically but needing to be "born again" spiritually, or in bondage and needing to be "saved."

In the famous parable of the prodigal son, a lad takes his financial inheritance even before his father dies and heads off to a far country where he wastes his life in riotous living. Broke, this wayward Jewish boy takes a demeaning job caring for a Gentile's pigs. The narrator tells us that the boy was eating pig slop when he uttered five magical words: "He came to his senses."

Every pilgrimage back to fully human begins when we come to our senses and realize that we have become less than human. Fourth-century theologian St. Augustine of Hippo wrote the first true autobiography in Western literature. In it he reflected on his journey from a life of sensuality, religious superstition, and empty careerism to a genuine spiritual awakening. He penned the famous words, "God has made us for Himself and our hearts are restless until they find their rest in God." Without God we are missing something essential to a complete and satisfying human existence.

Writer Douglas Coupland had an epiphany when he tried and failed to love his friends: "Now here is my secret. I tell it to you with an openness of heart that I doubt I shall ever achieve again, so I pray that you are in a quiet room as you hear these words. My secret is that I need God—I am sick and can no longer make it alone. I need God to help me give, because I no longer seem capable of giving; to help me be kind, as I no longer seem capable of kindness; to help me love, as I seem beyond able to love."[1]

Some spiritually restless people *feel* their way into the kingdom of God, others *think* their way there. Frederica Matthewes-Green tells the wonderful story of the Genoveses finding God. Eugene Genovese enjoyed a brilliant career as a historian, and his wife Elizabeth, also an academic, helped launch the feminist movement. Together they founded the magazine *Marxist Perspectives*, which is one of many reasons they were dubbed "the royal couple of the radical academic." But their intellectual curiosity and honesty led them down an unexpected path. Eugene tells the story.

> In the *Southern Front* I STILL spoke as an atheist; one reviewer said that I protest too much. When the book came off the press and I had to reread it, I started wrestling with the problem philosophically, and I lost. In the meantime, Betsey was going through her process, and one day announced she'd had a conversion. Now, she and I talk about religion a lot, but for six months we hadn't. So we were doing it separately.... On a philosophical level...what I came to decide was that being an atheist involves as great a leap of faith as being a theist. Deep down I think I knew that; it was just my preferred leap of faith. But I was troubled by this even as an undergraduate, when I read *The Brothers Karamazov* and encountered Ivan's question: "If there is no God, is not everything permissible?"[2]

Novelist Robert Stone, who had left religion twenty years earlier, awoke one morning feeling "half his head was missing" and began to hunger for God. Describing the situation to me he said, "You leave religion with a tremendous sense of liberation and then years later you discover that something really important is missing." He added, "There is the element of man, as Pascal said, 'The world everywhere gives evidence of a vanished God and man in all his actions gives evidence of a longing for that God.'"[3]

By the age of twenty-three, journalist Malcolm Muggeridge was a hard drinker and womanizer who nevertheless wrote to his father, "I want God to play tunes through me. He plays, but I, the reed, am out of tune." In 1958 he wrote in his diary: "Christianity, to me, is like a hopeless love affair. It is infinitely dear and infinitely unattainable. I...look at it constantly with sick longing." By 1966 he was a self-professed "religious maniac without a religion" who declared, "I don't believe in the resurrection of Christ, I don't believe that he was the Son of God in a Christian sense," and said he was "enchanted by a religion I cannot believe." Later he described how his journey to Christian faith came through the intellectual influence of seven spiritual thinkers: St. Augustine of Hippo, William Blake, Blaise Pascal, Leo Tolstoy, Fyodor Dostoevsky, Dietrich Bonhoeffer, and Søren Kierkegaard, whom he referred to as God's spies.[4] But his conversion also came through an encounter with Mother Teresa in whom he observed Jesus' teaching embodied in action.

Some people come to their senses through a mystical experience. As a young boy preparing for confirmation in the Episcopal Church, artist Bruce Herman was reading the Sermon on the Mount and came to the verse, "Blessed are the pure in heart for they shall see God." In that moment he received a foretaste of this when he was utterly engulfed in light—above, beside, below, and within—and experienced total peace and the assurance that all would be well. Some years later while pursuing Eastern mysticism under the tutelage of a guru in India, he realized that this man was an imposter and was not the light. Bruce knew this because he had seen the light as a boy. He began his journey back to God through Jesus.

In every case our opportunity for a new start begins when we recognize that something essential is missing intellectually, spiritually, morally, creatively, or relationally. Our very yearning to be more than we are is a wake-up call from God. It is our chance to "come to our senses." The Talmud tells the story of Rabbi Akiba, who on his deathbed worried aloud to his rabbi that he was a failure. His rabbi moved closer and asked why and Akiba confessed that he had not lived a life like Moses. The poor man began to cry, admitting he feared God's judgment. At this, his rabbi leaned into his ear and whispered gently, "God will not judge Akiba for not being Moses; God will judge Akiba for not being Akiba." Akiba was a man who sensed he was going to the grave with his song unsung and still in him. He had spent his life trying to be like Moses instead of simply becoming the best version of himself.

You are not being measured against other people; your success or failure is measured by what you have done with the unique capabilities and potential God designed into you. Some people pursue the spiritual without regard for becoming more human and other people seek to be fully human artistically, creatively, or intellectually, but not spiritually. Yet to become fully human and fully alive means becoming all you can be in order to exemplify God's greatness as your creator and designer.

All the metaphors for our renewal begin with "coming to our senses," with a new awareness, a moment when we awake from our sleep, are healed of our blindness, a moment when the contrast between what is and could be is crystal clear. The process always begins with a recognition and acknowledgment of our need, a turning from our current way of life and a dedication to a new life, a deep changing of our mind about the true nature of our situation.

Many of us can relate to stories of coming to our senses and becoming aware of our need for God. But, you may ask, what has all this to do with me? If you've never felt incomplete or longed for the transcendent, let me gently remind you that among the side effects of our dehumanizing disease are memory loss, drowsiness, and a euphoric sense of wellness even as we waste away in our illness. Some people have accepted a dehumanized existence as the only kind of life a human is capable of living. They believe brokenness and sickness unto death are simply the way things are and always will be, so we may as well "eat, drink, and be merry, for tomorrow we die."

Once a blind man came to Jesus for healing and the first question Jesus asked him was, "What would you like me to do for you?" The first time I read that story I thought Jesus' question didn't make any sense. Isn't it obvious that a blind man needs to see? However, I've come to realize that seeing requires that the blind person know and acknowledge his need for and possibility of seeing. The implication? We can be asleep, blind, spiritually dead, or in bondage and not even know it or accept it as inevitable! To you I say: "Come to your senses!"

When Joni Mitchell penned her famous lines about getting back to the garden she was writing as one whose memory of a better place had been awakened. When the Beatles told the wistful story of a girl leaving her parents after years of living alone, they were awake to our universal hunger for deep, caring relationships. Don Henley had a flash of insight into our loss of moral truth when he wrote the song *Garden of Allah* about expert witnesses lying at the O. J. Simpson trial. When art critic Brian Sewell bluntly derided the avant-garde gallery scene of the twentieth century's last decade, saying, "If this is art, I know no word that fits the work of Michelangelo and Titian," he was reflecting on the loss of the aesthetic of beauty and the degeneration of human creativity. When we learned that Tiger Woods, who excelled at golf, was a serial adulterer we cringed, because we intuitively know that true greatness requires a complete and whole life, not a compartmentalized one. We know it is not enough to reach our professional potential while ignoring our moral, intellectual, or spiritual life.

All around us are the personal and societal signs of human decline and each is a wake-up call to "come to our senses" and see our true situation. When war and violence break out in a nation or a home, when hatred reigns, when a child is abused, when tempers flare, when greed prevails, when our work is sloppy, when we exchange beauty for ugliness, when we resort to manipulation, deceit, or coercion instead of reason, when lust replaces love, when we put other gods ahead of the one true God, when human behavior reflects our fallenness instead of our better nature—all these are clattering alarms trying to awaken us from our slumbers. As Herman Melville declared in *Moby Dick:* "Heaven have mercy on us all, Presbyterians and Pagans alike, for we are all somehow dreadfully cracked about the head, and sadly need mending."[5]

When the prodigal hit bottom he came to his senses, arose, and went to his father. When you awaken to your human condition, fallen and broken, sick and dying, autonomous and isolated from God, consistently missing the mark, there is only one who can rehumanize you: God your creator and Father. Your pilgrimage back to God begins when you come to your senses and then return to the only one who can restore you to being fully alive and fully human.

9

returning

There are only three kinds of people:
Those who have found God and serve
Him; those who are busy seeking Him and
have not found Him; and those who live
without either seeking Him or finding Him.
—BLAISE PASCAL

So what are these people looking for?" Rachel was
dumbfounded when she learned that our little island
church is packed each Sunday. I told her our mission
at Orcas Island Community Church is "to pursue God in
the company of friends for the benefit of the world," and
I figure people are showing up because they want a connection with God, need to travel life's road with friends in

community, and like most everybody else on this island, have learned that serving each other is really important.

Rachel is a *real* islander—as in she's been here more than thirty years—and she also fits the Pacific Northwest religious profile: she is irreligious but considers herself spiritual. Yet, as so often happens in these conversations, I sensed something more than curiosity behind her question. This feeling was confirmed as she continued to bear down on the two words *pursuing God*.

"How do you pursue God?" she wondered aloud.

For some this is a religious question, or may be a philosophical one, but to me this is *the* essential human question. If it is true that we are created in God's image for a personal, intimate relationship with God, we can never be completely human without God. Every culture, tribe, language, and ethnicity tells stories of the relentless search for a transcendent being. French mathematician and philosopher Blaise Pascal spoke of a God-shaped vacuum in each human that can only be filled by God.

Some religions teach that God is unapproachable and unknowable, but the Bible reveals a God who wants to be found and known. Jesus made a comforting promise to the many seekers he met: *Ask and it will be given to you; seek and you will find; knock and the door will be opened to you.* Jesus understood a great mystery of the spiritual universe: We are not just seeking God; God is seeking us. Picture an injured climber stranded in a fresh, hastily dug snow cave as blizzard-like conditions descend upon the mountain. He stares at his GPS beacon, knowing that his only hope for survival depends on a rescue team being sent to find him. God is searching for those needing to be rescued and wanting to be found.

God in Search of Humans

When you come to your senses and know you are lost and dehumanized, you can be assured God the rescuer is looking for you. When you finally realize you are sick unto death, God the great physician is prepared to make a house call. When you awaken to your brokenness, God the restorer is on the way. The ancient Jewish stories all reveal God's persistent search for those who wish to find Him. After Adam rebelled, God called out, "Where are you, Adam?" and came and found him hiding in the garden. Later, when the "Lord saw how great man's wickedness on the earth had become, and that every inclination of the thoughts of his heart was only evil all the time," God sought out someone who was seeking him. He found Noah and through him saved humans from the great flood.

God set in motion a plan to reveal his love for all mankind through a man who lived in the ancient Sumerian city of Ur, declaring to Abraham, "Leave your country, your people, and your father's household and go to the land I will show you. I will make you into a great nation and I will bless you; I will make your name great, and you will be a blessing. I will bless those who bless you, and whoever curses you I will curse; and *all peoples on earth will be blessed through you.*"

The plan to bless all nations continued with Jesus, whom God sent not to condemn the world but to love and save the world. Jesus told stories about God seeking the lost, speaking metaphorically of a woman who searched diligently to find one lost coin, a shepherd who left the ninety-nine sheep in search of the one lost sheep, and the father who watched each day for his runaway wayward son to return.

Throughout all of human history, God, the seeker who wants to be found, has revealed glimpses of Himself, sometimes directly to humans, at other times through the written record of the prophets, and more generally through nature, which declares the glory and beneficent nature of God.

Seeking But Not Finding God

This brings us to the great paradox of America's spiritual journey: If God is everywhere and wants to be found, why do so few of us find God? Repeatedly, national surveys identify a large portion of Americans who declare they are spiritual seekers but apparently are not finding. In the decade I've been watching this phenomenon, the percentage of self-identified seekers has stayed firmly in the 82 percent range. So why are so few are finding? Pascal said, "There are only three kinds of people: Those who have found God and serve Him; those who are busy seeking Him and have not found Him; and those who live without either seeking Him or finding Him."[1]

Many people do not seek God. Atheists don't seek God because they have concluded there is no God to be found. Agnostics believe there is not enough evidence one way or the other to prove God's existence, but remain open to the possibility of God's existence. This openness is no substitute for genuinely seeking.

Some people seek but don't find because their search is superficial. In a day when "seeking" is in vogue, our culture has made it a primal value. Consequently, a generation of "seekaholics" seem content to seek and never find. Thus one bumper sticker declares, "The seeking is the goal and the search is the answer." Actress Meg Ryan captured this zeitgeist, saying, "I was raised a Catholic and it didn't work for me, and it's because it didn't work for me that I became a seeker. I love the word 'seeker' because that's what it says, that I have no answers, that I'm always in the questioning mode and it's my favorite thing to talk about."[2]

Other seekers lack the persistence and patience to find God. In his book *Bobos in Paradise: The New Upper Class and How They Got There*, journalist David Brooks jests about a baby boomer who meditates by a Montana river, looks at his watch, and realizes he had better start feeling a serene oneness with God's creation pretty soon because he has dinner reservations in Missoula at six o'clock.

Dispiriting doubts arising from devastating experiences in their own lives derail some earnest seekers. The birth of my brother with brain damage when I was ten and the death of C. S. Lewis's mother when he was eight are two examples of childhood experiences that can lead to doubt, disbelief, and a disinterest in pursuing God.

Sometimes people create their own custom-tailored God. In Robert Bellah's *Habits of the Heart*, Sheila Larson says, "I believe in God. I'm not a religious fanatic. I can't remember the last time I went to church. My faith has carried me a long way. It's Sheila-ism. Just my own little voice."[3] A long-ago *New Yorker* cartoon pictures an aging couple shaking hands with their priest as they leave church saying, "So long, Padre. Estelle and I have decided to set up our own little religion." If there is no God, creating one is understandable. But if there is a true, living, personal God, creating your own god is called idolatry. Sheila, as well as Estelle and husband, may no longer be seeking, but they have not found God.

Some people seek half-heartedly because they fear what will happen if they encounter the living God. C. S. Lewis admitted that for many years his search for God was insincere, confessing, "Amiable agnostics will talk cheerfully about 'man's search for God.' To me, as I then was, they might as well have talked about the mouse's search for the cat!"[4] Who would seek out and voluntarily enter into a relationship that will overwhelm and consume? What rebel wants to lay down his arms? Which people who relish doing things their way would seek out the Lord of the universe who requires them to yield to change their allegiance and their ways?

When I teach on spirituality I often start by asking if it is possible to be on a spiritual journey without religion.

I then ask if it is possible to be on a religious journey without searching for the spiritual. Finally I ask if the optimal path is a search for the spiritual within religion. I have found the latter to be true, agreeing with what novelist Rick Moody told me of his return to the church of his childhood after years of a "spiritual journey" outside of religion. He said, "Prior to my return to the Christian faith all my talk about the spiritual was kind of vague and squishy, but I came to realize there was no 'there, there.'"[5] We went on to agree that spirituality without religion is often rootless, and ignores centuries of wisdom. It is often individualistic, missing out on the camaraderie, encouragement, and accountability of community. It is often undemanding, allowing us to create our own God whose low expectations we are able to meet.

Finding God

Becoming fully alive and fully human starts with finding the living God, and finding God starts with believing there is a God who has revealed Himself and can be found if we seek Him. "You will seek the Lord your God, and you will find Him if you seek Him with all your heart and with all your soul" (Deuteronomy 4:29).

Finding God requires attentiveness to the clues all around us. God created us in His image so that as we see each other, even in our fallen state, we can get glimpses of God. God placed eternity in our hearts so that we would intuitively long for the eternal. God is revealed in the created order, the exquisite, complex, fascinating universe. In ancient days God spoke through the prophets. These all point to God but shouldn't be confused with God.

Some seekers commune with nature, believing the creation itself or Mother Earth is their God; others are obsessed with Scripture, believing that by mastering it they have found God. God has spoken through his imprint in our lives, through nature and through Scripture, but they are not God, they are communications from God. It is the God who communicates that we seek, not the means of communication.

A Matter of the Heart

Our search for God is a matter of the heart because this God we seek is a person, not just an idea or concept. During a particularly rough patch in my life there was a short period of time when I was alienated from my parents. There was no communication, no interest in relationship, and no desire for reconciliation. At the center of our disagreement were matters of the heart, and so it is with our search for God. God is a person from whom we are estranged and our search does not originate in our heads. An inquiring mind gratifies God, but it is an open, willing, hungry heart that draws God like a magnet because a true relationship begins in the heart.

Jesus consistently got to the heart of the matter: "The good man brings good things out of the good stored up in his heart, and the evil man brings evil things out of the evil stored up in his heart. For out of the overflow of his heart his mouth speaks." When the Lord saw the grieving widow, we are told, "his heart went out to her and he said, 'Don't cry.'" In the parable of the sower and the seed, Jesus says, "The seed on good soil stands for those with a noble and good heart, who hear the word, retain it, and by persevering produce a crop." Jesus commanded the disciples: "Love the Lord your God with all your heart and mind." We find God when we drop the barriers and open our heart to God.

Persistence

Only the persistent will find God. One windy night my wife heard noises and asked me to see what was going on. I went to the back deck and found a raccoon climbing onto a bird feeder. I shooed the masked bandit away and settled back into bed when she heard another sound coming from the kitchen. This time I found an open window with the breeze causing the curtains to flap against some objects on the windowsill. I shut the window and returned to bed, when Kathy heard yet another sound, this time coming from the front of the house. I sprang into action and found a spooked deer munching on some flowers on our porch. The deer scampered off. I figured having searched the back of the house, the front of the house, and the kitchen that my seeking and finding were done. But then my wife said she heard another sound. This time I discovered my daughter Molly's bedroom door gently opening and closing. I asked what was blowing, and Molly answered astutely and half-asleep, "The air." I shut her bedroom window, closed her door firmly, and finally, having searched and found, went to sleep.

Our search for God requires an ongoing tenacity because those who seek will find God, and those who find God will always realize there is more about God to be discovered and more of themselves to make known to God. As St. Benedict prayed, "It is Christ I am seeking, and it is Christ who is seeking me, the Whole Christ seeking the whole me." Hunger and thirst, knock, seek and ask, and ye shall find, said Jesus.

Reunion

In the story of the prodigal son, the wayward son comes to his senses, returns to his father, and asks forgiveness for his rebellious departure. Similarly, our return to God reunites us with the person who knows us best and loves us, but who is also deserving of an apology. When my parents and I reconciled, the first step was renewed communication. The same is true with God. After we are reunited with God the process of getting reacquainted begins, and this happens in a variety of ways.

John Wesley taught that God's revelation is confirmed in four primary ways: *Scripture*, the written revelation of God; *the Church*, God's revelation interpreted in community; *personal experience*, God's revelation confirmed in your life; and *reason*, God's revelation confirmed in your thinking.

You can know God more intimately as you study the Bible because it is a written revelation of God's identity.

There you will see that God is creative, spiritual, intelligent, communicative, wise, infinite, sovereign, holy, omniscient, faithful, love, omnipotent, self-existent, self-sufficient, just, immutable, merciful, eternal, good, gracious, and omnipresent. As your life becomes centered in God you will see those qualities affirmed in your own experience with God. As you enjoy fellowship with a community of fellow pursuers of God, you will learn more about God through the experience of others.

But ultimately, we do not seek to know *about God;* we seek to *know and experience God.* The successful seeker will be attentive to God's presence in daily life. The Bible says that Jesus rose up a great while before the day and went out alone to pray, and almost without exception my own day starts with quietness, meditation, prayer—the reading of Scripture and a variety of devotional books. These first moments of the day allow me to calibrate my will to God's and set the tone for attentiveness to God throughout the day.

Prayer is the most basic and essential way we know and communicate with God. I remember meeting with a group of irreligious guys who were seeking to find God. At the end of one of the sessions I asked if any of them would like to talk to God. One of them, Larry, looked at me like I was an alien from outer space. "Talk to God? You mean out loud?" he blurted out. He had always believed in God but had never actually talked to God!

The apostle Paul recommended that we talk to God (that is, pray) without ceasing. In other words, you can communicate with God each moment of the day, silently or aloud. For people just learning to pray I often recommend reading and praying through the Book of Psalms, because most of the Psalms are transcriptions of prayers that can help us communicate with God.

The psalmist reveals a hunger to know God: "Show me your ways, O Lord; teach me your paths. Lead me in your truth and teach me, for you are the God of my salvation; on you I wait all the day" (Psalm 25:4–5).

In the Psalms we read the great confession of King David after he committed adultery: "Have mercy on me, O God, according to your steadfast love; according to your abundant mercy blot out my transgressions. Wash me thoroughly from my iniquity, and cleanse me from my sin. Wash me, and I shall be whiter than snow. Let me hear joy and gladness. Hide your face from my sins, and blot out all my iniquities. Create in me a clean heart, O God, and put a new and right spirit within me. Do not cast me away from your presence, and do not take your Holy Spirit from me."

In the Psalms you'll read anguished cries for help: "Save me, O God, for the waters have come up to my neck. I sink in the miry depths, where there is no foothold. I have come into the deep waters; the floods engulf me. I am worn out calling for help; my throat is parched. My eyes fail, looking for my God. Those who hate me without reason outnumber the hairs of my head; many are my enemies without cause" (Psalm 69).

The psalmist is not afraid to express his anger at God in his prayers: "My God, my God, why have you forsaken me? Why are you so far from saving me, so far from the words of my groaning?" (Psalm 22:1). "Awake, O Lord! Why do you sleep? Rouse yourself! Do not reject us forever. Why do you hide your face and forget our misery and oppression?" (Psalm 44:23–24).

You know you are developing a relationship with God when you find yourself communicating with God honestly and continuously when you rise in the morning, throughout the day into the evening, and even when you awaken in the middle of the night!

Aglow with God

Picture your life as a kerosene lantern. The glass is blackened with soot so that even if you could light it, the flame could not be seen through the grime. Imagine now that all the essential elements of the lantern are there—the brass frame, the side glass, the wick, the fuel container in the base, and a ventilated cover on the top. It is obvious that it is a lantern, but it will not start and cannot offer the light and warm glow one expects from a lantern.

When you displace God from the center of your life the contours of your human capacities are all there, mentally, creatively, relationally, morally, and spiritually, but the glass is darkened and the essential fuel of God's presence is missing. When you are reunited with God the fuel is in place and the lantern is set to glow again with God's presence. When God is restored to the central place in your life, you regain the possibility of bringing glory to God by becoming fully the person who God created you uniquely to be. The evidence of seekers who find is the restored glow at the center of their lives; it is like an unplugged lamp that is plugged in again, the car out of gas that is refueled and starts again, the flashlight with new batteries that sends a beam of light once more.

Two things are necessary to return to and find God. God must reach out to you and you must reach out to God. The apostle Paul described this transaction beautifully when he said, "By grace you have been saved through faith." God's grace is God reaching out to you; your faith is you reaching out to God. You have come to your senses, you have returned to God your creator by faith.

God is the creator of life and God is the giver of new life. Before you can be fully human, you must be fully alive, and before you can be fully alive, you must be awakened from the dead.

10

awaking from the dead

Die? I should say not, dear fellow.
No Barrymore would allow such a
conventional thing to happen.
—JOHN BARRYMORE

n the movie *Sixth Sense* young Cole Sear (Haley Joel Osment) utters the famous line, "I see dead people." Child psychologist Malcolm Crow (Bruce Willis) asks Cole if he is referring to seeing dead people in his dreams. No, says young Cole, he sees dead people while he is awake, and they are walking around like regular people. They're not in graves or coffins; they are everywhere, and he sees them all the time.

This is the best way to describe how God sees us. When a condemned prisoner is led to execution, the guard leading the prisoner to his death calls out, "Dead man walking; dead man walking here." Spiritually, we are all dead men walking, because although we may be physically alive, our sickness unto death is causing our spiritual condition to deteriorate further each day. Needless to say, a dead person is incapable of being fully human and fully alive!

It is difficult for us to grasp our spiritual deadness because we often hide our soul sickness well. But sooner or later the revelation of our true condition is unmasked. In the summer of 2009 the nation witnessed the very public humiliation of Governor Mark Sanford. He had disappeared for a few days, claiming that he had been hiking the Appalachian Trail, but then under pressure he confessed that he had been out of the country—in Argentina, visiting his mistress. One of Sanford's friends was not surprised and commented, "For too long, I think, Mark has been dead on the inside."[1]

This came on the heels of the news of presidential candidate John Edwards's betrayal of his wife, Elizabeth, and then reports in the book *Game Change* that Elizabeth was an abusive, intrusive, paranoid, condescending, crazy woman—nothing like her image as St. Elizabeth. When the authors interviewed Edwards's former staffers, the nearly universal assessment among them was that "there was no one on the national stage for whom the disparity between public image and private reality was [more] vast or more disturbing."[2]

These highly visible personalities reveal publicly what we know to be true privately among the rank and file of everyday humans. Behind the masks of social acceptability lurk dark pockets of decay in each of our lives. We've all known people who felt "dead inside," and the truth is at one time or another most of us have been that person. The loss of a child or a devastating illness can make you feel dead inside. Victims of sexual, physical, or emotional abuse know what it means to feel dead inside, as do people whose lives have unraveled because of addictions. Lonely people in the throes of divorce or separation or hungering for love and intimacy but not finding it know the feeling of being dead inside.

Our spiritual decay spreads to every part of our lives and through us to the culture we create and sustain. Peruse the shelves of your local bookstore and you'll find myriad books about the death of art, the death of civilization, the death of reason, or the death of basic human decency. Watch today's films and you'll see stories of humans who are dying a slow death that is playing out in their lives, work, and families. Turn to the world of games and you'll find a horror/fantasy, role-playing game called *Dead Inside*, which is based on characters who have lost their souls or were born without souls. A Web site called the *Experience Project* features a chat room for people who want to tell their stories of feeling dead inside. There you read the sad tales of men and women who feel numb and lifeless and are trying to decide whether getting up each morning is worth it.

As we've already seen, this sickness unto death is universal and pervasive, and it has a corrosive effect on every aspect of our lives. Thus when the apostle Paul said, "You are dead in your trespasses and sins," he was simply affirming something about ourselves that we already knew.

When you come to your senses and realize your predicament you may be tempted to mount a vigorous self-improvement campaign. You may swing into action, reading self-help books, attending self-improvement classes, joining a group for people whose addictions mirror yours. You may attend church, read the Bible, change your diet. All these are wonderful action steps, but think about this: Is a dead person really improveable in any significant way? No! To the contrary, dead people don't need improvement; they need life!

Most of us are familiar with the old spiritual, Dry Bones. You know:

> The toe bone's connected to the heel bone.
> The heel bone's connected to the foot bone.
> The foot bone's connected to the leg bone.
> The leg bone's connected to the knee bone.
> The knee bone's connected to the thigh bone.
> O, hear the word of the Lord! Dem bones, dem bones gonna walk aroun'.

These lyrics tell the story of Ezekiel's vision of a valley full of dry bones. Ezekiel was a Jewish prophet who witnessed the exile of Jews in Babylonian captivity and was distressed because he saw his nation and culture dying. In Ezekiel's vision God revealed that these dry bones represented the nation of Israel whose hope was gone.[3] But God also told Ezekiel he planned to open the graves and bring Israel back to life.

This story is a metaphor for the spiritually dead. God asks Ezekiel an important question: "Son of man, can these bones live?" He is asking whether or not the spiritually dead can be revived. For you and me this is not a theoretical, abstract question; it has personal consequences because remember, when God sees us, God sees dead people!

Can dry, dead bones come back to life? Is spiritual death the end? Is our physical death the end? Are any humans beyond redemption? Can our sickness unto death not be healed? Are there dying relationships that cannot be brought back to life? Can fallen humans be restored to being fully human?

Can these bones live? Ezekiel was humbled by his inadequacy to answer God's question and replied, "O Sovereign Lord, you alone know." God *does* know, and the answer is clearly good news. God tells Ezekiel that the dead, dry bones *can* come back to life, and soon, in special effects that James Cameron would envy, there was a noise, a rattling sound, and the bones came together, bone to bone. The bones were reassembled, but still there was no life in them.

This is analogous to what happens when we try to rebuild our lives without God. Self-help can reconstruct the essential elements of our life, but as Ezekiel was about to learn, only God can breathe new life into the reassembled bones and make them dance. "The Sovereign Lord says to these bones: 'I will make breath enter you, and you will come to life. I will attach tendons to you and make flesh come upon you and cover you with skin; I will put breath in you, and you will come to life. Then you will know that I am the Lord. . . . I will put my Spirit in you and you will live, and I will settle you in your own land. Then you will know that I the Lord have spoken and I have done it,' declares the Lord."

This is a metaphor for our human dilemma. Our sickness unto death has tarnished God's image in our lives. We've been diminished spiritually, intellectually, creatively, relationally, and morally. Try as we may to regain fullness of life, our best efforts are never enough. Yet spiritually dead people can be brought to life; the fallen human can get a fresh start. Dry bones can be reinvigorated. But there is a caveat. Jesus said it best: "With man this is impossible, but not with God; all things are possible with God. . . . For nothing is impossible with God. . . . What is impossible with men is possible with God" (Matthew 19:26). When it comes to our spiritual death, only God can bring us back to life.

When Jesus came to earth he saw people who were dead on the inside, so he offered them new life. Jesus proved he could awaken the dead when he literally raised Lazarus of Bethany from the dead by simply saying the word.[4] When Jesus arrived on the scene, Lazarus had already been dead and in the tomb for four days. "Jesus called in a loud voice, 'Lazarus, come out!' The dead man came out, his hands and feet wrapped with strips of linen, and a cloth around his face." The story of Lazarus is interesting not just because it shows Jesus' power to revive the dead but also because it teaches us three lessons about *how* God wakes the dead.

The first lesson we learn is that while only God can actually wake the dead, the process must begin with a dead person who wants to be brought to life. Lazarus had to follow Jesus' command to "come out."

In the same way, before you or I can be made into a new human and begin the journey from fallen human to fully human, we must desire a new life and take appropriate action. There comes a time when you must acknowledge that doing things your way has led to your sickness unto death and you cannot resuscitate yourself. This is not an easy thing to admit. The same pride that caused Adam to break from God is still at work in us today. We don't want to yield our life to God. We don't want to admit that without God we are the equivalent of dry, dead bones. Humans are masters of a blinding self-deception. John Barrymore's last words before he died were, "Die? I should say not, dear fellow. No Barrymore would allow such a conventional thing to happen."

You can choose to refuse God's offer of life, but if you do, you will be the lesser for it, and so will the world. We all need to hear your song sung fully and heartily. Recently, I heard the story of a group of young cellists gathered for a master class with the brilliant Yo-Yo Ma. During the class, Ma led the young cellists into a deeper understanding of their instruments, their music, and themselves. At one point a young man finished playing a movement of Brahms' cello sonata, and Ma said, "Nobody else can make the sound you make." This was meant as a compliment to the young man. It was true for everyone in the class and it is true of you. Nobody else can make the sound you make.

When we come to our senses and return to the Father, God is ready to meet us. My friend Brian had been doing things his own way for years until he faced prostate cancer. He attended church on Christmas Eve for the first time in ages and kept coming back for more. One Sunday after church he called me at home and said, "Something is happening to me. During the sermon my heart felt warm and my resistance to God is all melting away. We need to talk!" I went and spent a few hours with him and his wife, answered their questions, prayed with them, and left. About a week later I saw Brian at a vintage car show and he looked irritated. He said to me, "I feel like you led me up to the water and didn't show me how to drink it." I laughed, saying he sounded downright biblical. I pointed out to him that Jesus used the same metaphor, offering his seekers springs of living water and the bread of life! Brian had come to his senses and was ready for new life, but wanted to know how it could happen.

I told Brian that Jesus used a whole cluster of words to describe the path to newness of life and I told him what they were.[5] But I also told him that Jesus summarized his message quite simply, "If anyone loves me, he will obey my teaching. My Father will love him, and we will come to him and make our home with him" (John 14:23). When God takes up residence in our lives, he offers to invigorate every fiber of our being—not just spiritually but also creatively, intellectually, relationally, and morally. New life is ours when the giver of life dwells within us, making us fully alive.

The second lesson we learn in the story of Lazarus is that though Jesus is the life giver, he involves other people in the process of bringing the dead to life. The scene is actually rather comical. As Lazarus came out of the grave he was entangled in the entrapments of death, "His hands and feet were wrapped with strips of linen, and there was a cloth around his face." This reminds us that in addition to Lazarus's desire to be freed from his bondage, there were aspects of his release that required the help of his friends. Before Lazarus could come out of the grave his friends had to "take away the stone." When Lazarus emerged tangled in the death garments, Jesus asked his friends to free him: "Take off the grave clothes and let him go."

The first thing Jesus does when he awakens us from the dead and gives us new life is to remind us that we have been made for camaraderie and collaboration with one another. We are together again! You can't take your grave clothes off by yourself! The same creator who gave Eve to Adam to help him has given us each other to help us grow from the newness of life to a fully human life. This book grows out of my experience with hundreds of people who influenced my life to help me become more fully human. Art Miller and Ralph Mattson; my grandmother; my parents; my brother; teachers, professors, mentors, authors, philosophers, filmmakers, theologians, songwriters; my wife and my kids—the list is endless. Your life too will be shaped by your friends for the journey; invite them in, listen to them, watch them, break bread with them, serve them, and love them, and together with them grow toward a fully alive and fully human life.

The third lesson this story teaches us is that Jesus is the giver of new life. Jesus once said, "I am the way, the truth, and the life, no one comes to the Father except through me" (John 14:6). When you come to your senses, when you return to God, you will discover that there is only one who can show you what being fully spiritual and fully human looks like. This one has paved the way for us to become fully human. God sent him to earth specifically to begin the process of restoring all that unraveled in the fall. His name is Jesus, he is fully God and fully human, and he is uniquely the great humanizer.

V

progressing to fully human

making all things new

11

the humanizing jesus

Jesus didn't come to make us Christian;
Jesus came to make us fully human.
—HANS ROOKMAAKER

As a young boy and pastor's son, I was exposed to a Christianity that was fearful of culture. We were forbidden to engage in worldly practices like dancing, going to the movies or live theater, swearing, playing cards, smoking, drinking, or playing football on Sundays. As for me, a rebellious little snot, I danced the Bunny Hop at a second grade party, was sent to the principal's office for swearing in the fourth grade, snuck out to a movie and took my first sip of Scotch by age twelve, strutted by the folks at church wearing mud-soaked clothes after playing football on a rainy Sunday afternoon, and tried my first cigarette at fifteen, all the while believing that at any time the foreordained wrath of God would crash down on my wee little reprobate head. I was living proof that fundamentalism breeds hypocrisy.

When I was a teen I recall my dad talking to my mom about making a change to pastor in a different, more culturally suitable church denomination because he felt like a cultural misfit in ours. My dad dearly loved the culturally diverse group of people in the church he pastored, but he wondered if someone else would be more effective with them, and often he was frustrated with the "anti-intellectual culture" of his denomination. Personally, he was a student of English literature and enjoyed listening to Bach, Beethoven, Mozart, and Mahler, but he was serving in a culture of good-hearted folks who for the most part frowned on "secular literature" and favored the Bill Gaither Trio and gospel quartets to classical music. Years later I heard that one of the bright lights of our denomination, A. W. Tozer, once visited Fuller Seminary and when asked what he was reading replied, "Karl Barth, but don't tell the folks in my church back home." Why are people with active minds and a refined aesthetic sometimes made to feel these qualities are out of sync with being Christian?

The denomination of my youth was very concerned about sharing the gospel with primitive tribes in foreign lands. One of the highlights of the year was the annual week when missionaries would come and dance the native dances, play samples of indigenous music, and prepare exotic meals typical of the culture they served. As a very young boy I remember consciously asking why they could celebrate those cultures while we were supposed to steer clear of our own. Even as kid I wondered if people in these cultures, should they decide to become Christian, would be asked to abandon their dances, music, and interesting foods for a blander, less "worldly," less human life. It made me sad to think they might. I wanted to live life fully and felt that being Christian required painting life from a limited, less vivid, less vibrant palette of colors.

The gospel I heard as a child was that God loves us, but we are sinners who have disobeyed God and are deserving of hell. Jesus died to pay the price for our sins so we could go to heaven when we die. The job of the Christian was to be a good person and share with other people how they could become a Christian. The world was divided into "us" and "them," and we were to avoid spending too much time with "them" except when we were very intentional about trying to get "them" to become one of us.

I moved to the San Francisco Bay Area to attend college in the 1960s during the peak of what is now recognized as a seismic cultural revolution. They say if you remember the 1960s you weren't actually there, but I was there and I recall the attraction of the emerging provocative music, literature, and films of the era. My curiosity drove me into the cultural scene where I saw the excess and abuses of "sex, drugs, and rock 'n' roll" atop what at the same time was a spiritual, questing youth culture.

I visited churches and discovered a broader cultural palette than the one I had been raised in. I observed what sociologist Peter Berger describes as three broad worship traditions within American Christianity. Some were highly propositional, focusing on teaching. Others, like the Pentecostal or African American gospel churches, were highly experiential. A third group (Roman Catholic, Episcopalian) focused on the sacraments and the mystery of the faith. I wondered why all three could not be found in each house of worship. Why must one choose between teaching, experience, and awe?

In the '60s churches were also in upheaval, generally reacting to the long-haired, hippie, pot-smoking generation in one of two ways. They either recoiled in shock and horror, circling the wagons to keep the good guys in and the bad guys out, or they tried to be hip and relevant, taking on many of the faddish ways of the era. I wondered whatever happened to the idea of being in the world but not of the world? Whatever happened to the simplicity of pursuing God in the company of friends for the benefit of the world?

It was a confusing time. I recognized the good and bad of both my church upbringing and the chaotic culture around me, and neither seemed to offer a solid foundation for building my life. I took my questions to my grandmother Cora, who in addition to making an incredible homemade apple pie with a slice of sharp cheddar cheese on the side, was an intellectually curious, independent thinking spirit, and who had always loved me despite my penchant for coloring outside the lines in wilder, brighter colors.

Her simple advice changed my life. She told me I should read the gospels and get acquainted with who Jesus was in his culture as a way of sorting out who I should be in mine.

So I read the gospels word by word for the first time. The most obvious and surprising revelation was the Jesus I encountered. This Jesus who jumped off the pages was a radical thinker who was actively present in his culture (not withdrawn from it), was a loving presence (not hostile), and was a transforming presence in his culture (not a conformist). He clearly marched to the beat of a different drum. And I was relieved to see he did not carry the baggage associated with the religion that bears his name. He did not demonize, alienate, and demean fallen people; he loved them. He revealed to everybody—from the smug religious types like Pharisees to social and religious outcasts like prostitutes and drunkards—that there was a more abundant and full life available to them now, not just in the future.

Jesus had a humanizing effect on his disciples' lives. Those early followers of "the way" out-thought, out-lived, and out-died their pagan counterparts. For centuries thereafter it was Christians who created a better and richer culture, writing the best music, creating the best art, and cultivating a rigorously intellectual life. They also rolled up their sleeves and served society in practical ways, providing care for the physically infirm, offering community to the lonely outsiders and financial assistance to the poor. They pursued science as a way of understanding the universe and harmonized their theology to fit the facts they discovered in their no-holds-barred scientific inquiry. It became obvious to me that Jesus calls us not to become entrapped in religious practices that make us less human but rather to a dynamic, zestful, fully alive and fully human experience. Followers of Jesus are expected to live holistically, developing all our capacities. In our daily life we should put on display the creative, intelligent, spiritual, communicative, purposeful qualities God endowed us with uniquely when we were created in God's image. Our corporate worship should synergistically engage the intellect, reflect the verve of those who encounter and experience the God of the universe, and also explore the sacramental mysteries of God. Jesus didn't come to narrow our lives, he came to broaden them.

To live a fully alive, fully human life became my personal aim, and quite honestly it has continued to mean generally being out of step with both the culture and the church of my time. I take comfort in knowing that this is what Jesus experienced as well. Around the time I first had these realizations, I heard a phrase that described my emerging understanding of what I was discovering about Jesus. Art historian Hans Rookmaaker, a colleague of Francis Schaeffer, said, "Jesus didn't come to make us Christian; Jesus came to make us fully human."

This idea, if true, has radical implications. It means that becoming authentically and fully human is the evidence of being a true follower of Jesus. It means that the question we should ask is not, "Are you a Christian?" Instead, the more important question is, "Are you becoming more fully human?" The question is not, "Are you going to heaven when you die?" Instead, the question is, "Are you living a fully human life now?" The question is not, "How successful are you at avoiding the world?" The question is, "How effective are you as a loving, transforming presence in the world?"

How Is Jesus the Great Humanizer?

I came to see Jesus as the great humanizer. I realized that he did not come to start a new religion; he came to rehumanize dehumanized humans, to restore the luster of God's image so we can again glow with God's holistic presence spiritually, intellectually, creatively, morally, and relationally. Jesus came to earth to restore fallen humans to fully human beings regardless of their ethnicity, nationality, gender, and economic, educational, or social status. Jesus was not a Westerner who came to earth for Christians, and though a Middle Eastern Jew, he did not come to earth just for Jews. Jesus came for every human on earth. Frederick Frank once asked, "Could the meaning of being born human be to become human?"[1] The answer, of course, is yes! The humanizing hope Jesus offers is for all humans everywhere, because all humans everywhere are created by God and in God's image.

Though Jesus Is God, He Became Fully Human

When God became human in the person of Jesus Christ, who is both fully God and fully man, God affirmed human existence and signaled his intention of restoring humankind, not destroying it. Some in the first centuries were shocked at this news, so ready were they to disown the flesh. The incarnation, or enfleshment, of God in Jesus settled that issue once and for all. It is not the body that is evil, the fallen will and deeds of humans who inhabit the body are evil. So committed to the flesh is God that we are

promised a new resurrection body when Christ returns. This
is what Eugene Peterson means when he says:

> Matter is real. Flesh is good. Without a firm rooting
> in creation, religion is always drifting off into some
> kind of pious sentimentalism or sophisticated intel-
> lectualism. The task of salvation is not to refine us
> into pure spirits so that we will not be cumbered
> with this too solid flesh. We are not angels nor are
> we to become angels. The Word did not become a
> good idea, or a numinous feeling, or a moral aspira-
> tion; the Word became flesh.[2]

Jesus is fully God and fully human and this has clear
implications for all humans. We must reject attempts to
diminish our spiritual nature to elevate our human nature,
but we must also resist attempts at diminishing our human
nature in order to elevate our spiritual nature. Jesus intends
that we will be both fully alive spiritually and fully human.
It is God's intention that our human nature be made complete spiritually and our spiritual nature be made complete
in the flesh.

As Creator of the World, Jesus Is Uniquely Qualified to Re-Create Us

Jesus was more than a great teacher or prophet. The apostle
John reminds us, "In the beginning was the Word, and the
Word was with God, and the Word was God. And the Word
became flesh and lived among us." Do you follow what is
being said here?

The creator of the universe has stepped into our human story on planet earth to re-create humans so that we can once again reflect God's image as it was meant to be from the beginning. As the ancient church father St. Athanasius said, "The renewal of creation has been wrought by the self-same Word who made it in the beginning. There is thus no inconsistency between creation and salvation, for the One Father has employed the same agent for both works, effecting the salvation of the world through the same Word Who made it in the beginning."[3]

God has not discarded us or forgotten our potential. As a child, I was taught that salvation was about redeeming me from my sins so I could have a future in heaven. This is a true but incomplete statement. Jesus coming in the flesh reminds us that we were "created beings" before we were fallen beings, and we were created beings before we were "redeemed" beings. God has not given up on his original intentions for us at creation. Redeeming us does not involve rejecting our humanity; it involves remaking and rehumanizing us.

Though he is perfect, Jesus loves fallen humans. In his *Screwtape Letters* author C. S. Lewis marvels at God's love and creates the fictional demon Screwtape who warns his understudy, "We [demons] must never forget what is the most repellent and inexplicable trait in our enemy [God]; He really loves the hairless bipeds."[4] The good news is that Jesus has come to restore all that unraveled in the fall. God loves us the way we are but loves us too much to leave us the way we are in our fallen, shattered, sickened state. In Jesus Christ humans get a new chance.

Jesus Showed Us What Being Fully Human Looks Like

Jesus' authenticity and vibrant humanness attracted people and intrigued them. By being who God created him to be through reflecting God's image and by doing God's will, Jesus glorified God. He reflected God's image in one human life, just as Adam should have done. Likewise, we do not glorify God by "becoming a Christian," we glorify God by become fully who God created us to be. Becoming more like Jesus does not just mean becoming more spiritual; it also means becoming more fully human! This is what early church father St. Irenaeus meant when he said, "The glory of God is man fully alive." Jesus glorified God by being fully alive and showed us what a whole, complete, fully human life looks like in the flesh. His intellect, creativity, spirit, relationships, and morality were reminders of what God created humans to be. We can see God's image shine through each dimension of Jesus' life, and taken together they form the complete, well person. Jesus personified the wholeness of the Hebrew *shalom* and the Greek *arête* to which we aspire.

Intelligent   In the gospels we read an account of Jesus amazing the rabbis with his insight and intelligence as a twelve-year-old boy. "After three days they found him in the temple courts, sitting among the teachers, listening to them and asking them questions. Everyone who heard him was amazed at his understanding and his answers" (Luke 2:47). When he began his public ministry people were "amazed at his teaching, because he taught as one who had authority, and not as their teachers of the law" (Mark 1:22). Jesus taught his followers to love God with their mind, confirming that to be fully human means to use our mind fully.

Creative   The apostle John said that Jesus participated in creating the world and the apostle Paul adds, "All things were created by him and for him." Such creativity manifested itself when Jesus took on flesh. He turned water into wine at the wedding at Cana and fed the five thousand with a few loaves and fishes. His creativity was revealed in the masterful development and presentation of extraordinary parables that are as fresh and compelling today as they were two thousand years ago. He lived a Technicolor life in a black-and-white world and showed his followers that to be fully human is to exercise your creativity in daily life.

Spiritual   Jesus, full of the Holy Spirit, returned from the Jordan and was led by the Spirit in the desert. Jesus returned to Galilee in the power of the Spirit. Jesus nurtured an intimate relationship with God, often getting up early in the morning so he could worship, pray, and seek God's will for that day. Jesus taught his followers to worship in spirit. Jesus promised that the Holy Spirit would indwell his followers. Jesus was the personification of the spiritual life in the human life and set the standard for his followers; to be fully human is to nurture our spiritual capacity each day.

Relational   From the moment his public ministry began
Jesus was fully engaged in relationships. He called twelve
disciples to be with him 24/7 for three years. He stopped
along the way and conversed with people religious and
irreligious alike. He sat at Greco-Roman meals engaging
in provocative discussions with the cultural elite. He
welcomed little children. He spoke to crowds of five
thousand, yet also had time for the lonely blind man at the
side of the road. The man of solitude was a man for the
people and of the people. It was clear to Jesus' disciples
that love is the essence of our faith and love is lived out
in relationship; to be fully human is to be relational.

Morally Exemplary   Jesus said, "Do not think that I have
come to abolish the Law or the Prophets; I have not come to
abolish them but to fulfill them" (Matthew 5:17). Humans
trapped in sin serve themselves, behave in dehumanizing
ways, and are in bondage to behaviors they cannot stop.
Jesus' allegiance was to God and his daily behavior reflected
a complete submission and obedience to God's will on earth
as it is in heaven. The writer of Hebrews states emphatically
that Jesus was without sin. And so Jesus' followers seek to live
morally upright lives. Yet the apostle John catches the tension
of fallen humans as we grow towards fully human when he
said, "If we claim to have fellowship with him yet walk in
the darkness, we lie and do not live by the truth. If we claim
to be without sin, we deceive ourselves and the truth is not
in us. If we confess our sins, he is faithful and just and will

forgive us our sins and purify us from all unrighteousness"
(1 John 1:6–9). We are the grateful recipients of God's mercy,
grace, and forgiveness when we fail, but we realize that to
be fully human is to live morally in ways that please God.

Jesus Succeeded Where Adam and Eve Failed

Jesus showed us that the flesh can be fully inhabited by the
Spirit. As a matter of fact, Jesus showed us that becoming
fully human requires becoming fully spiritual. When Jesus
took on flesh he waded into the brokenness and sickness of
Adam's estranged and alienated mind, yet he did so victori-
ously. Each day of his thirty-three years of life in the flesh
Jesus fought a war with the Adamic nature and was tempted
in every way every other human is, yet was without sin. He
showed how a human who seeks and does the will of the
Father can enter the fellowship and camaraderie of Father,
Son, and Holy Spirit while here on earth. It all starts with the
daily prayer, "Thy will be done on earth as it is in heaven."

Athanasius captured the significance of the incarnation when he said, "God became man so that man
might become like God." Athanasius didn't think humans
would literally become God, but he did believe that
because of Jesus we could again reflect the godlikeness
of God's image imprinted on our life. The good news of
the incarnation is this: in Jesus, the Spirit of God dwelled
in human flesh and for those who follow Jesus, the flesh, the
human body, can again become the dwelling place of God.
Jesus came to reverse all that unraveled in the fall.

In Jesus' Death, the Grip of Adam's Fall Is Ended

We were suffering from the metastasized cancer called sin. It deserved the death penalty. The dilemma God faced was how to kill the cancer without killing the humans created in His image whom He loves. The solution was for Jesus to carry the Adamic nature to the cross so God Himself could undo the catastrophe of Adam's rebellion and fall. In Jesus' fully human life we saw what Adam could have been; in Jesus' death, the grip of Adam's lineage is loosened, our death sentence is lifted, and we have a chance to start over in our calling to do God's will each day and thereby become the full reflection of God's image in our lives. Paul put it like this, "For Christ's love compels us, because we are convinced that one died for all, and therefore all died. He died for all, that those who live should no longer live for themselves, but for him who died for them and was raised again."

In Jesus' Resurrection, God's Power Over Death Is Revealed

Jesus' death on the cross was his final refusal to be bound by Adam's destiny of fallenness in this world, nor was he prepared to accept death as the end of human life. Followers of Jesus no longer fear death because its power has been defeated; nothing, not even death, will separate us from the love of God.

Jesus' ascension means we have an advocate with God now for we are told that Jesus has ascended into heaven and sits at Father God's right hand. A human being, a Jew, a son of Adam, and the divine Son of God incarnate, is face to face with the Father and is advocating on our behalf.

I learned the importance of advocacy on a trip to Washington, D.C. Charlton Heston was the speaker at a luncheon. When he finished he skipped out a side door. Late for my next appointment I slipped out the same door right behind him but security guards immediately stepped in to stop me from using this private, celebrity exit. Heston turned, and recognizing me from interviews we had done together in Chicago, laughed and said, "Don't worry, guys, he's with me." Because of him I was allowed through. Because Jesus knows his followers and we are with him, we have unrestricted access to God.

The Beginning of a New Kind of Human Race

Because we were trapped in the sickness unto death that is the aftermath of Adam's fall, our only way out of bondage was for Adam's race to die and a new race to be brought to life. At Jesus' crucifixion, the first Adam died. At Jesus' resurrection, a new race of Adams was given life. The crucified and risen Jesus offers a fresh start to anyone prepared to deny the first Adam's nature and to follow the living Jesus instead. Fallen humans can become fully human because of Jesus, who as a son of Adam and the Son of Heaven paved the way for us to end Adam's reign in our life by all becoming children of heaven.

The death of the first Adam and the hope of life in the lineage of a second Adam is at the heart of the good news of Jesus as described in the New Testament and it is the basis for Hans Rookmaaker's phrase: "Jesus didn't come to make us Christian; Jesus came to make us fully human." Inquiring minds want to know: Does it say this somewhere in the Bible or is Dick Staub just making this up? Let me show the flow of New Testament teaching that underscores this point.

We die because of Adam; we have new life because of Jesus. Our human lineage is in Adam; our spiritual lineage begins with Jesus, the last Adam. Jesus' resurrection makes him the firstborn from the dead and the beginning of a new race of humans. The firstborn of a new creation perfectly reflects the image of God. Jesus is the fullness of God and because of him we are fully reconciled to God and are no longer alienated from God. Jesus came to begin a new race of humans.[5]

All this can be summarized this way: Jesus didn't come to make us better people, he came to make us *new people*. Jesus offered his followers an abundant life, which means a full and complete life. He came to make you fully human, to enable you to become the best version of yourself. Succeeding at this involves a lifelong process of allowing Jesus to restore the luster of God's image in every aspect of your life. Because Jesus alone lived such a life, Jesus alone is qualified to restore you to such a life. In your fallenness the image of God has faded, the shattered masterpiece in you needs restoration. But the good news is that Jesus can restore your soul, renew your mind, rekindle your creativity, reform your morality, and rebuild your relationships.

12

restoring

We are God's workmanship, God's *poem.*
—APOSTLE PAUL

On *Antiques Road Show* hapless mere mortals line up with their most precious possessions hoping theirs is a masterpiece that has been languishing in the attic or basement all these years. Occasionally the expert will spy a genuine work of art beneath the surface of a painting dulled by dust and grime, or a piece of furniture will turn out to be rare and valuable though marred by a mottled finish on a side panel, or a vase will be deemed the work of a master glass artist and of great worth despite the slight crack developing along the base.

In each case the owner is immediately admonished to take the work to a professional restorer. They are always warned that under no circumstances should they try to restore it themselves. "Doing it yourself will only make matters worse," they are told. Many an amateur has ruined a valuable painting or piece of antique furniture with their attempt at cleanup and touch-up. It takes patience, skill, and experience to restore a masterpiece to its grandeur.

This is an apt metaphor for your situation, for you are a masterpiece crafted by God even though you have been damaged and marred by the fall. God's image is hidden beneath layers of dust and grime. Your spiritual, intellectual, creative, moral, and relational capacities are beneath the surface, waiting to be restored to their original luster. But now that you are alive and have returned to God, who is qualified to bring forth the best version of yourself?

Jesus is the master restorer of your potential. Given our metaphor it is interesting that it was an art historian, Hans Rookmaaker, who recognized the radical truth that "Jesus didn't come to make you Christian; Jesus came to make you fully human." Immediately after you return to God, you are given a new life, and God sets in motion a plan to restore and remake you into a new person.

I have a confession to make. Through my daughter Molly I've gotten hooked on HGTV. I especially like the home remodeling projects where the homeowner has in mind remodeling an existing home and is told by the contractor that a "teardown" would be preferable. In other words, the contractor is saying that "it is not possible to fix what you've got, you'd better tear it down and start all over."

This is the best way to describe our situation. We know how things are supposed to be. From the beginning we were created in God's image with unique spiritual, mental, creative, relational, and moral capacities. It was God's intention for us to enjoy an optimal life in a delightful environment well-suited for our development as fully alive, fully human creatures.

We know how things are. Though we try to overcome the effects of our sickness unto death, we've all missed the mark, pledged allegiance to ourselves instead of God, and engaged in behaviors that are unloving toward others and diminish ourselves. Once we come to our senses and return to God, we desire to rediscover what it means to be restored to a fully human life. Now comes the staggering news that the restorer has in mind a rather extensive makeover. God intends to make all things new. To use our builder's analogy, we don't need a remodel, we need to start over. The path to being fully alive and fully human is not by way of becoming better people; instead, it requires becoming a new kind of human.

God loves to make things new. Read the Hebrew scriptures and you'll see the pattern: new wine, new grain, new king, new clay, new house, new altar, and a new song. Where God reigns, something totally new arises. When Jesus arrived he began to make things new: a new covenant, new commandment, new teaching, new life, and new self. This is thrilling news once you realize you need a makeover, because the master craftsman of all time is going to accept the job. Good things are going to happen!

A Whole New Person

The teardown has begun and the new construction is under way. Now that you are alive the restoration of God's image can begin. Though God is the only one who can transform you, your restoration is a collaborative venture with you and God. The apostle Paul said it this way, "Continue to work out your salvation with fear and trembling, for it is God who works in you to will and to act according to his good purpose" (Philippians 2:12–13). Just as scissors with one blade cannot cut paper, the process toward becoming human requires two blades—you and God. Here are some of the ways God will change your life when you decide to become the fully human person, the best version of yourself, that He intends you to be.

A New Heart

One of the most dramatic promises God makes is this one: "I will give you a new heart and put a new spirit in you; I will remove from you your heart of stone and give you a heart of flesh" (Ezekiel 36:26). Jesus confirmed that his followers would have a change of heart, "For out of the heart comes evil thoughts, murder, adultery, sexual immorality, but the seed on good soil stands for those with a noble and good heart" (Luke 8:15).

God gives us a fresh start when he creates a clean heart in us. Our new heart is variously described as pure, humble, serving, generous, faithful, discerning, glad, devoted to God, responsive to God, tested and found true, moved by God, upright, joyful, trusting, broken, contrite, undivided, wise, steadfast, free, and obedient. Our new heart loves and obeys God and its affections are on things above, not on earthly things. Because of this new heart we are the grateful recipients of God's surpassing love, but we are also carriers of God's love to everyone in our life.

It is one thing to desire a new heart; it is another matter to cultivate one. Dallas Willard rightly refers to the cultivation of a new heart as a renovation that involves a lifelong process of taking the daily and often small steps to our inner transformation. *If you want to be the best version of yourself, fully alive and fully human, you will ask God to create in you a pure heart of love and devotion for God and you will take the steps necessary to allow God to accomplish that work.*

A New Mind

Jesus said there are two basic minds: the mind focused on the things of God and the mind focused on the things of man. The apostle Paul was one the first century's leading intellectuals; nevertheless, when he became a follower of Jesus he described the contrast between his mind before and after God. The mind of sinful man is death, but the mind controlled by the Spirit is life and peace. Before Christ our minds are confused, anxious, cunning, evil, troubled, terrified, depraved, corrupt, hostile to God, and unspiritual.

Paul said God restores your mind so that you will be in your right mind. Your new mind seeks to know the mind of the Lord and is a steadfast and peaceful mind, a keen mind full of knowledge and understanding, a spiritual mind. The prophets prayed for such a mind saying, "Test me, O Lord, and try me, examine my heart and my mind."

Your new heart makes you willing to change, but your mind is the center of your transformation. The apostle Paul put it this way, "Do not conform any longer to the pattern of this world, but be transformed by the renewing of your mind." The word transform in Greek literally means "metamorphosis"— the process of the caterpillar transforming into the butterfly. For years your mind has been patterned to think in certain ways by the fallen world around you. Your mind must be renewed so it will not just confirm to those old deeply engrained patterns. Only as your mind is renewed will you be able to test and approve what God's will is—His good, pleasing, and perfect will.

Renewing your mind involves knowing and understanding God's ways and then applying what you've learned in everyday life. Your new mind will differ from your old mind in what you think about, how you think about it, and what you do about it.

God has crafted your mind with aptitudes that you must fully develop. Some minds are analytical, others intuitive, some gravitate toward ideas, and others toward numbers. Harvard University's Howard Gardner has identified eight kinds of smarts: linguistic intelligence ("word smart"), logical-mathematical intelligence ("number/reasoning smart"), spatial intelligence ("picture smart"), bodily-kinesthetic intelligence ("body smart"), musical intelligence ("music smart"), interpersonal intelligence ("people smart"), intrapersonal intelligence ("self smart"), and naturalist intelligence ("nature smart").[1] God designed each of us with distinctive ways of learning and thinking, so your potential is reached only when you develop your individual capacities. You will learn in your own distinct way, because God designed you with specific optimal ways of learning. Every follower of Jesus wants to increase in his or her knowledge of the faith through the word of God, but how do you learn? Some of us learn by listening and would have done well when God's words were passed down as an oral tradition to be memorized. Other people learn by reading and enjoy sitting alone with their Bible having a "quiet time" each day. Some people are collaborative learners who love processing their thoughts with other people in small groups. Some people are hands-on learners who acquire knowledge by doing. *If you want to be the best version of yourself, fully alive and fully human, you will develop your mental capacity to its fullest.*

A New Spirit

The apostle Paul taught that the acts of the sinful nature are obvious: sexual immorality, impurity, and debauchery; idolatry and witchcraft; hatred, discord, jealousy, fits of rage, selfish ambition, dissensions, factions, and envy; drunkenness, orgies; and so forth. He warned that no one who lives like this can inherit the kingdom of God.

By way of contrast, the spirit of the new kind of human is characterized by love, joy, peace, patience, kindness, goodness, faithfulness, gentleness, and self-control. The Holy Spirit, who dwells within you when you invite God to rule your life, produces this new spirit. Anytime your old spirit manifests itself (in fits of anger, a lack of self-control, or lust, for example) you know you are not allowing God's Holy Spirit to rule your life. Nurturing your spiritual self involves understanding God's expectations, listening to your conscience, and yielding your will to God each moment of each day.

All who seek to nurture their spiritual nature will experience resistance, for the same evil one who enticed Adam and Eve is still at work today. Your old Adamic nature is seeking to overthrow your new spiritual nature, and this struggle is not against flesh and blood but rather against the powers of this dark world and the spiritual forces of evil. The apostle Paul used the metaphor of the warrior's armor to describe the weapons you can use to win this war. They include:

> Be strong in the Lord and in the strength of his
> power. Put on the *whole armor of God*, so that you may
> be able to stand against the wiles of the devil. For
> our struggle is not against enemies of blood
> and flesh, but against the rulers, against the authori-
> ties, against the cosmic powers of this present
> darkness, against the spiritual forces of evil in the
> heavenly places. Therefore take up the *whole armor of
> God*, so that you may be able to withstand on that
> evil day, and having done everything, to stand firm.
> Stand therefore, and fasten the belt of *truth* around

your waist, and put on the breastplate of *righteousness*.
As shoes for your feet put on whatever will make you
ready to *proclaim* the gospel of peace. With all of these,
take the shield of *faith*, with which you will be able
to quench all the flaming arrows of the evil one. Take
the *helmet of salvation*, and the *sword of the Spirit, which is the
word of God. Pray in the Spirit* at all times in every prayer
and supplication. To that end *keep alert* and always *perse-
vere in supplication* for all the saints (Ephesians 6:10–18).

Many people mistakenly think the Eastern religions
have the corner on cultivating deep spirituality, but the fact
is that a remnant of Christianity has always maintained deep
traditions for cultivating spirituality through meditation,
solitude, simple living, prayer, fasting, reading, silence, and
worship. *If you want to be the best version of yourself, fully alive and fully
human, you will develop your spiritual capacity to its fullest.*

New Relationships

You are made for relationships, but chances are your relationships will be one of the areas of your life requiring the
biggest changes. I say this because, before enthroning God,
most people are living self-directed lives. The self-directed
life is the source of tension in every relationship, because
two selves wanting satisfaction will always be at war; every
self wishes to impose its wishes on the other. This is especially an issue in marriage because the aim of this union
is to make one new self of two selves. This is possible only
when each self yields. Since the 1960s the culturally
accepted mantra is to be ourselves, fulfill ourselves, do it

our way. Is it any wonder that this generation is known for high divorce rates? Pope John Paul II identified the problem when he said, "In a self-seeking age, marriage degenerates from the mutual love of husband and wife into two loves of self, two loves existing side by side, until they end in separation."

Tension with your parents, siblings, neighbors, coworkers, and spouse, or with your own children, is almost always rooted in the clash of two self wills. The way out is love, acceptance, and forgiveness. Jesus said his new commandment was that we love one another and that love was the evidence that someone is his follower. Loving other people requires learning to forgive them, and this is why Jesus taught his disciples to forgive even their enemies. It takes strength, not weakness, to forgive and the easiest way to eliminate an enemy is to forgive an enemy. *If you want to be the best version of yourself, fully alive and fully human, you will develop your relationships to their fullest, allowing God to change you and freeing you to love, accept, and forgive others.*

Full Expression of Your Unique Creativity

Many religions aim at eliminating individuality, but the Christian faith celebrates the expression of your uniqueness. Becoming the best version of yourself will require your uniqueness to be expressed in what you make with your talents, because who and what you can become is defined by your unique gifts, talents, and temperament. This means you should discover what you do well and enjoy doing and then do it for God's glory.

Not all are called to be creative artists in the specific sense of the term, yet all men and women are entrusted with the task of crafting their own lives, making them works of art, masterpieces. The apostle Paul said we are God's workmanship and the word he uses for workmanship is *poeme*, the root of the word for poem. You are God's poem written in the kind of life you live and what you do with your time and talents. You have been crafted with the potential to create work only you are capable of. God made you unique and takes pleasure in your uniqueness, so your best way of showing that God is central in your life is by developing who God made you to be to the best of your ability. *If you want to be the best version of yourself, fully alive and fully human, you will identify, develop, and express the unique God-given talents God has entrusted in your care.*

Rhythm and Balance

God designed our planet with a certain rhythm. On earth we experience a 24-hour day, a 7-day week, and a 365-day year. Though every human has the same amount of time, each of us manages how we will use our time. By setting aside a Sabbath day, an entire day for rest, and by setting our biological clocks for sleep at night, God signaled the human need for sleep, rest, and play. Just as fields produce better crops when they are allowed to lie fallow on occasion, so human lives are most productive when they master the art of rhythm and rest.

C. S. Lewis was known for his productivity, but according to Lewis scholar Paul Clasper, it was Lewis's sense of balance and his proper priorities that made him productive.

> The English style of spirituality is a rhythm of wor-
> ship, work, reading, and leisure. This is an un-frantic
> response to God who is, as Lewis insisted, always a
> courteous Lord. Life-style is revealed by the use of
> time: what is given place and space; what is included
> and what, therefore, is excluded. What we see in
> Lewis is the steady place of his parish church; the
> quiet regularity of his Bible-reading and prayers;
> the natural large place for his main work of study
> and writing; the large blocks of time for leisurely
> conversations with special friends; and the impor-
> tance of letter writing, especially with those who
> sought his help in the matter of Christian pilgrim-
> age. For all of his immense output of literary work,
> his life is marked by a spacious, un-frantic rhythm
> of worship, work, conversation, availability, and
> intimacy.[2]

For a recovering workaholic like me, this is an ongoing challenge. When you are young you work hard to achieve the right opportunities, and then, as you get older, you may find yourself with a surplus of amazing opportunities. You can't do everything, so which activities will you choose? Working more hours or longer is not the solution, because God's desire is for you to live a balanced and holistic life. Allowing your closest friends, and if you are married, including your spouse in your decision-making process, is essential. If you want to be the best version of yourself, fully alive and fully human, with help, you will establish a balance and rhythm in your daily life.

Wholeness

Perhaps the biggest challenge you will face is synthesizing all the elements of your life into one whole person. For years I excelled in my career by allocating a disproportionate amount of time to my work, often to the detriment of my family life. My life of the mind and enthusiasm for ideas and concepts have often come at the expense of my relationships with people. Picture yourself as an orchestra that sounds good only when all the various elements are playing in harmony and in sync. The score of music from which each player reads, and the conductor each player watches and follows, ensure the possibility of a harmonic, well-timed, beautiful sound. When God is central in our life, God writes the score; we are God's poems. *If you want to be the best version of yourself, fully alive and fully human, you will allow God to be the conductor who pulls together the different elements of your life into a harmonious whole.*

Take the Leap

Ralph Waldo Emerson said, "We are very near greatness; one step and we are safe; can we not take the leap?" I am encouraging you to take the leap, to become the fullest expression of your best self, to allow God to develop in you a warm heart, a keen mind, a settled, deepened spirit, a distinct creativity all your own, and an expanding circle of healthy relationships and to bring a healthy balance in your life so you can live it fully and healthily.

Because your life experiences and personality are unique to you, when you decide to take the leap your journey with God will be your own. The person with a rough past may discover that though he is through with his past, his past is not through with him. A tenderhearted person may need a tougher, more disciplined heart, and the unsympathetic person may need to be tenderized. The person who gravitates toward ideas may need to rely more on the spirit, and the intuitive person who thrives on excitement and exuberant experiences may need to enhance her life of the mind and the disciplines of silence and solitude. The naturally gregarious person may need to spend time in solitude, and the loner will be called into deeper relationships.

In each case, the path to your fullest development requires the holistic and synergistic transformation of your spirit, mind, creativity, and relationships. It will also require that as each aspect of your life is fully developed it will be done in harmony with all the other dimensions of your life. Like the Greeks we should aspire to *arête,* becoming a complete, well-balanced person who is fully mature—body, mind, and spirit. Like the Hebrews we aspire to *shalom,* a wellness and wholeness.

It is never too late to become the complete, whole person God created you to be.

What is the fire within you? *Fan it into a blaze for God's glory.*

What is your song unsung? *Sing it for God's glory.*

What is your heart's desire? *Pursue it.*

What do you need to see changed in your life? *Ask God to change it.*

13

your design, your destiny

There are no ordinary people. You have
never talked to a mere mortal.
—C. S. LEWIS

When you decide to become the best version of
yourself, your desire to make the best use of your
talents will become more purposeful. Theologian
Frederick Buechner offers this advice, "The kind of work
God usually calls you to is the kind of work that you need
most to do and that the world most needs to have done. The
place God calls you is the place where your deep gladness
and the world's deep hunger meet."

In my experience, discovering how God designed you
is essential for finding your deep gladness and for fulfilling
your destiny, for your destiny is woven into the uniqueness

of who you are. What you are supposed to do with your life is written within you by God, who designed you to enjoy and do certain things well. You just need to discover who God made you to be and then express your irrepressible uniqueness in daily life! My personal process of discovering my unique God-given design started back in 1979 when two distinguished-looking men from Connecticut walked into my office, threw their Brooks Brothers topcoats over a chair, and changed my life.

Art Miller and Ralph Mattson had just published a book titled *The Truth About You*. After thirty years of preparing in-depth assessments of a diverse pool of over thirty-thousand people, they had made some important discoveries. First, each person they interviewed possessed a cluster of unique abilities. Second, each person worked best in certain circumstances, when dealing with certain subject matters, and while relating to other people in a certain way. More important, they were each motivated to use those abilities to accomplish a specific purpose.

Art and Ralph identified five dimensions—motivation, abilities, subject matter, circumstances, and operating relationship with other people—and found that taken together these dimensions formed a distinct, integrated pattern. They observed that when examined in detail, no two patterns were identical. Furthermore, each person's pattern emerged early in life and expressed itself irresistibly and irrepressibly. The more I listened to them the more I became convinced that they were describing a process that reveals the distinctive elements of God's image imprinted on each person.

They had found a way to identify God's handiwork as it is uniquely crafted in each of us.

Art and Ralph told me that most people do not harness their unique talent, but instead try to conform to the expectations of their parents, spouse, society, their teachers, their peers, or the dictates of their manager, company, or industry. Many people ignore the irrepressible genius within them and instead fall into the trap of believing they can become anything they desire to be simply by taking classes, reading books, or trying harder. So the daughter who hates math becomes an accountant because her accountant dad says it will offer steady work, or the shy son who can't stand talking in public tries to become a teacher because that is where the jobs are and it is a noble cause, or the team player tries to become a manager because that is the way to the top. I understood exactly what they were talking about. I had been convinced by a friend and mentor to leave a Ph.D. program in communications for a fast track in management. By the time I met Art and Ralph, I had managed people in both a large corporate and a not-for-profit setting. I was successful but frustrated in my work.

Using their sophisticated system for identifying what individuals do well and enjoy doing, Art gathered information about my specific enjoyable accomplishments and then produced an individualized, customized *motivated abilities pattern* (MAP) to guide me toward work that celebrated rather than suppressed the person God made me to be. By revealing my unique MAP, they showed me why what I was doing professionally was a good fit, but not the best fit, for me.

Once I got a clearer sense of my own uniqueness, I set about tailoring my life and work to better express the way God made me. I moved out of day-in, day-out management and into broadcasting as an on-air radio talk show host. The difference was remarkable! I had always been passionate about my work, but now my energy was focused not just on good work but on the best kind of work for me.

The same thing can happen to you. When you discover who you are and find a more suitable way to express it, you will experience a greater sense of fulfillment, because you will release the unique image of God within you more fully.

Your Unique Design Is Good

Earlier I said God is the great artist, but God is more than an artist; God is the *master* artist: "And God saw everything that God had made, and behold, it was very good" (Genesis 1:31).

God is a craftsmanlike creator, with an eye for detail, the techniques of the master, the attentive ear, the steady hand, the fertile mind, and an eternal palette of color and limitless library of sound. God is the baseline, plumb line, gold standard, muse, fountain, and source of all human creativity. You are the handiwork of this creator God, the great artist, the one who consistently does all things well, the one whose work is always brilliant and good. When God made you He said, "It is good."

This means, of course, that you should focus on discovering and expressing the hidden masterpiece that *you are* instead of being frustrated about who you aren't! It also means you'll need to see and honor the greatness and potential in others. This was one of Jesus' great gifts. He saw the potential in each person he encountered, helping them see how far they were falling short of their potential and then calling them to a full, abundant life. He reawakened latent spiritual, creative, intelligent, moral, and relational capacities. He specialized in summoning forth the best in people, and that is what he wants to do for you.

You Can Discover Your Design

Doing what you have been created to do is how you come fully alive. As Dr. Howard Thurman, dean of theology at Boston University, once said, "Don't ask yourself what the world needs. Ask yourself what makes you come alive and then go do that. Because what the world needs is people who have come alive."

The good news is that the process of discovering your design is simple. There are some excellent books to help you go deeper than I will here, and you can also seek out a professional trained to help you discover your unique design.[1]

Let me describe the process as I experienced it. I started by examining my life from childhood through to the present and identified in each period those achievements I did well and enjoyed doing. I then selected the most significant achievements from each period of my life and wrote a brief one-page summary of each, describing in detail how I went about achieving it. I was then interviewed for a couple of hours by a caseworker who delved more deeply into specifically how I went about accomplishing each of my achievements. The caseworker was not asking me psychological questions like why I did certain things or how I felt about doing certain things. Instead he concentrated on the details involved in the doing. My written comments along with the transcript of the interview were then forwarded to an analyst who produced the written report. After receiving the report and reading it I met for another few hours with Art, who helped me understand and interpret my MAP.

It would be an understatement to say that this document changed my life. Wise men have said, "Know thyself and to thine own self be true." You cannot be true to God's design on your life if you do not know what that design is. Knowing how God has designed you is your most important task if you want to be the fullest expression of God's image imprinted in your life.

Understanding Your Design

I have spent considerable time referring to my MAP throughout my life as a way to keep on track and understand when and how I get off track. It truly takes a lifetime to know yourself, and as your circumstances change in life, or when you find yourself feeling frustrated about your life and work, your MAP is a good place to start investigating the reasons.

To help communicate how understanding your design can be useful, at the risk of seeming self-important, I'd like to share my MAP with you just to give you a flavor of how it has helped me. You'll find the at-a-glance summary report attached as a footnote, but I'll refer to a few specific examples here.[2]

My MAP did not so much reveal things I did not know about myself as confirm things I knew about myself and showed how they fit with everything else in my design. You'll notice under the Motivated Abilities section it shows that I learn by reading and studying and that I communicate through articulating and explaining. Under Subject Matter you'll see ideas, concepts, knowledge, information, thoughts, and their expression. Now look under Motivating Circumstances; you'll see I like to see practical application of these ideas where there are difficulties, obstacles, tests, and challenges. Writing this book about the concept "Jesus didn't come to make us Christian; Jesus came to make us fully human" shows all these aspects of my design at play. I prepared to write this book by gathering information, reading, and studying the subject. *About You* is my way of explaining my thoughts and expressing the important ideas and concepts I've learned. I am trying to do it in a way that shows their practicality in everyday life. There are challenges, tests, and obstacles to writing a book. For one, I am busy with other things and have had difficulty carving out adequate time to think and write. Then, as I wrote this book I encountered issues about the subject that I needed to resolve. The fact that I am enamored with ideas means

I can get wrapped up in a conceptual world without bringing the concepts down to earth, so I had to work with an editor who let me know when I was being unclear.

So given the obstacles, why would I write a book? Look under my Central Thrust and you'll see that my primary motivational drive is to have an impact on people (or organizations or events) by building and developing and extracting potential. I believe the concepts I am sharing can help you achieve your potential, so I've tried to develop this book in a way that will make a mark in your thinking and your life for the good. You'll notice under Subject Matter that people, general, and people, individuals, are listed. This means that I'm a "people person," but the rest of the pattern says what I want to do with people: I want to influence them by expressing the thoughts and ideas that have been most useful to me in ways that will serve them.

When you look under Operating Relationship with Others you'll learn something about the way I relate to people in an organizational setting. I operate as an individualist but in a team context. Because I am entrepreneurial (see Suggested Function, and under Motivating Circumstances, growth, potential, new and different). I have usually provided leadership in start-up situations where I function as what MAP calls a "directive spearhead." This means I march into unknown territory and direct a team of people toward building and developing something that emerges from our journey into the unknown. Once things are established, you need a manager, not a directive spearhead, and that is the time I need to step out of the situation or modify my role.

I have taken time to show you some bits of my MAP to illustrate how useful knowing your God-given design can be for you. The truth about you is that you possess a unique design that is a guide to helping you radiate God's image as imprinted in your life. Once you identify your own MAP you'll be able to identify the situations where you can best glorify God by expressing who God made you to be.

The Death, Burial, and Resurrection of Your Design

Many people are excited to learn more about themselves so they can become more fulfilled in their lives. Your design is crafted by God and was in place in your life when you were a fallen human, serving yourself and not God. When you restore God to the central place in your life, your design doesn't change, but you will experience a change in your reasons for expressing yourself and in your desire to express yourself excellently and fully. No longer will you see your design as your unique possession for your satisfaction and personal benefit. You will realize that God's image is imprinted in you so you can bring God the glory through serving others. You will learn that your enjoyment and personal fulfillment is the by-product of the gifts you've received from God.

I like to think of this as a process of the death, burial, and resurrection of my design, my MAP. When I first discovered how God had designed me, I was tempted to become self-absorbed, constantly trying to understand and express my uniqueness, frustrated when I encountered situations where that did not seem possible. An immense amount of energy was being expended in this process until I realized that just as Jesus asked me to offer myself to him as a living sacrifice, Jesus was now asking me to offer my unique gifts and their expression in work back to him as well. This is what Rich Mullins describes in his song "Road to Damascus." He talks about his success and fortune and how they had become the source of his personal impoverishment. Then, like the apostle Paul on the road to Damascus, he encounters God and realizes that he needs to offer everything back to God. It was only then that he fully realized that everything he had to offer God *came* from God! There is a humility that arises when you allow your unique wonderfulness to die and be raised anew. Only when you've given it all back to God will you experience more fully the joy of understanding and expressing God's gifts imprinted uniquely in you.

Become the Masterpiece You Are Meant to Be

Michelangelo's masterpiece, the statue of David, was crafted from a piece of castaway marble so ruined it was deemed of no value by other artists. Michelangelo saw in it what no one else could see. He saw shape and texture and beauty in what everyone else discarded; he could visualize the statue of David in that odd-shaped stone. He once said his job as an artist was to release David from the stone, and that is what he did.

There are many masterpieces waiting to be discovered. During the 2009 NBA playoffs, a seven-year-old autistic child named Gina Marie Incandela sang the national anthem. This little girl had the type of powerful voice you would expect from someone at least three times her age and three times her size. Gina Marie had been diagnosed with autism just before she turned two. She could not even speak until she was three. Because she had trouble forming words, her parents sent her to a school for kids with special needs. Through music therapy she found her voice. The teachers released Gina Marie from the stone.

You may think of yourself as a piece of castaway stone of little value, or you may see your value but believe no one else does. The truth about you is that you can still become God's masterpiece if you will allow God, the master craftsman, to release you from the stone. In a sense every human is a special-needs kid. We all possess exquisite latent capacities because we are created in God's image. We all know what it feels like to be discarded and set aside as if we have little to offer. We all long for a Michelangelo to release us from the stone. Our sense of frustration when we are not fully who we can be is rooted in our understanding, conscious or not, that we are created by God and in God's image and therefore have incalculable worth.

C. S. Lewis put it this way, "There are no ordinary people. You have never talked to a mere mortal. Nations, cultures, arts, civilizations—these are mortal, and their life is to ours as the life of a gnat. But it is immortals whom we joke with, work with, marry, snub, and exploit—immortal horrors or everlasting splendors. Next to the Blessed Sacrament itself, your neighbor is the holiest object presented to your senses."[3]

When God wanted a temple built he called on the best craftsmen of the day. We're told that Bezalel and Oholiab were filled with the Spirit of God, with skill, ability, and knowledge in all kinds of crafts, to make artistic designs for work in gold, silver, and bronze, to cut and set stones, to work in wood, and to engage in all kinds of artistic craftsmanship. God filled them with skill to teach others and to do all kinds of work as craftsmen, designers, embroiderers in blue, purple, and scarlet yarn and fine linen, and weavers—all of them master craftsmen and designers. In this description we see the holistic nature of someone who is fully human: wise, creative, spiritual, and able to relate to others and to teach.

If you want to be the best version of yourself, fully alive and fully human, you will start by identifying and developing your unique, God-given talents to their fullest, and you will allow God to release you from the stone so you can do the craftsmanlike work you have been uniquely calibrated to do.

Recall that earlier we talked about Abraham Maslow, who believed our greatest happiness comes when we are self-actualized, when we reach the point in life where we have fully developed our moral, creative, and intelligent capacities. As you will see in the next chapter, your actualization begins now and is completed in eternity with God. For with God, our progress toward fully alive, fully human begins in this life and is completed in the next.

14

and in the end, a beginning

Aim at heaven and you will get earth thrown in. Aim at earth and you get neither.

—C. S. LEWIS

illiam Shakespeare's play *All's Well That Ends Well* is categorized as one of his problem plays because it cannot be neatly classified as tragedy or comedy; it is both. This is an apt description of our quest for the fully alive, fully human experience. We yearn for wholeness and completeness, yet we know what it means to take two steps forward and three steps back. As we advance and retreat through blue sky and mud, though our progress is at times tragic and at others comedic, Shakespeare's conclusion applies: as long as things end well, the ups and downs along the way are offset by the good outcome. Julian of Norwich's spiritual pilgrimage taught her that with God "all shall be well, and all shall be well, and all manner of things shall be well." We cling to this hope.

We want our spiritual, intellectual, creative, relational, and moral wellness to function synergistically so our wellness reflects the wholeness, balance, and harmony God intends.

We are looking for holistic completeness that restores wellness to our souls, minds, and creativity, that resets our moral compass and improves our relationships. We aim for *spiritual wellness* even in the toughest of times, as described in the old hymn "When Peace Like a River." We need the *mental wellness* that comes when a mind is renewed, such as occurred when Jesus healed the demoniac and the man was "clothed and in his right mind." We aspire to *creative wellness*, where our work is good, true, and beautiful and flows from God and back to God. This is what John Updike meant when he said, "I feel I am closest to God when writing. You're singing praises. You're describing the world, as it is. And even if the passages turn out sordid or depressing, there's something holy about the truth." We want the *relational wellness* attained by the prodigal son and his father. We want the *moral wellness* described by the psalmist who compares the happiness of the morally well and the unhappiness of the "wicked" saying, "Happy is the man who does not walk in the counsel of the wicked or stand in the way of sinners or sit in the seat of mockers. But his delight is in the law of the Lord, and on his law he meditates day and night. He is like a tree planted by streams of water, which yields its fruit in season and whose leaf does not wither. Whatever he does prospers. Not so the wicked! They are like chaff that the wind blows away."

As we aspire to our full humanness, we realize we live in the clash between the now and the not yet, and this tension produces deep longings for a completeness that seems just beyond our reach. C. S. Lewis explained the meaning of this longing, "If I find in myself a desire which no experience in this world can satisfy, the most probable explanation is that I was made for another world."[1] Paradoxically, the closer you come to the full actualization of your potential, the more you will realize its ultimate fulfillment is in the future. We are dying in the midst of living, like the majestic fir tree stretching skyward as its dead branches arch to the ground. Young or old, we look for the rungs of the ladder to take us on the upward path to the fully human life that will be ours perfectly in another world called heaven. So here are some practical suggestions to guide you on your way.

Start Now

Your spiritual capacity and eternal nature is clothed in flesh, but this is the place you begin your journey. Teddy Roosevelt's sister Corrine saw her brother overcome multiple obstacles in his life and it inspired her to urge people like you to "stretch out your hand and take the world's wide gift of joy and beauty."[2] The wonders of the world are within your grasp, but you must begin to pursue them or you will never attain them.

Remember Your Creator

The universe is immense and complex beyond our comprehension. The Hubble telescope brings back photographs
of the distant, expanding universe, and a new generation of
submarines plunge deeper into the previously unseen
oceans, discovering new exotic creatures. Fingerprints of
an infinitely creative God are everywhere, including in the
unique capacities woven into every human. Be embold-
ened each day with the thought that you've been crafted
to enjoy and do certain things exceptionally well, and then
pursue them and do them well. Don't allow the discovery
of your extraordinary gifts to draw you away from God.
But recognize with each achievement that these gifts came
to you from creator God and your handiwork can be presented to him as your gift of gratitude. Take Elizabeth Barrett
Browning's advice and see how earth is crammed with
heaven and God is ablaze in the common bush.

Know, Express, and Be True to Yourself

Listen to the guide within you as it prompts and nudges
you in new directions. Take the risk of examining yourself
and then seek out what makes you deeply alive. When you
discover the "real" you, develop and express who you are as
much as you can each day. Seek the closest correspondence
between the inner you and the outer you that other people

see and know. Don't be alarmed at the greatness of another human; rather, celebrate that person's genius and develop your own. Conformity stunts the growth of the true person and leads to a monotonous sameness. We are most fully human when the differences between us become clearer and we are able to collaborate more fully.

Become Who You Can Become Within the Boundaries of Your Reality

At the outset of this book I told you that when I was ten years old my brother Timmy was born with brain damage, leaving him unable to walk, talk, feed, or care for himself. At the time I asked if my brother's life had meaning. What is a fully human life, and could he ever live one?

In fact when I was in college my brother taught me one of life's most important lessons. I was home for winter break during my freshman year of college. Like many new college students I had exercised my newfound freedom irresponsibly and as a result of misallocation of time (that is, partying and playing instead of studying), I found myself ill-prepared for my upcoming finals. One day my parents asked me to care for my brother who by this time was eight years old. While I was reading the Bible (trying to get my life back on track), my brother crawled over to me, rose up on his knees, grabbed both my arms, and tried to say the word *brother*; it came out *bruv*, and was accompanied by a huge grin. In that moment I realized my brother was doing the absolute best he could within the boundaries of his limitations while I was squandering the abilities God had given me to walk, talk, think, read, and communicate. Within the confines of who he was, my brother was working each day to become the best version of himself that he could. His life had meaning, and he was living it fully within the context of his capacities.

Each of us has limitations by virtue of the gifts and capacities God has given us, and by virtue of the place and time in which we live. Our calling is to become the best version of ourselves that we can become, overcoming limitations when possible, operating as fully as possible within those limitations when that is our only option. This is what Holocaust survivor and psychologist Viktor Frankl learned in a Nazi concentration camp: even in the confinements of prison his life could have meaning, if he said yes to life each day and made the best of his horrific situation.

Make It Good—Aim High

I sat with a professional artist as he described showing his portfolio to a master artist he hoped would accept him as a student. Since youth he had always excelled in his art and after a steady diet of compliments and rave reviews by family and friends, he was a tad cocky. Deep within himself, though, he knew he needed to be better, but he didn't know how to get there. The master quietly studied the artist's portfolio and was silent for a very, very long time. He finally announced, "You've got a lot of talent, but not enough skill." Thus began this artist's hard, daily march toward becoming the best he could be, a journey that will not end as long as he is on this earth. Flannery O'Conner once remarked something to the effect that Christian writers "should be much less concerned with saving the world than with saving their work." If it is true, as experts have said, that it takes ten thousand hours to get really good at anything, it will take a lifetime to make ourselves into the masterpiece God intends for us to be. We should press forward seeking constant improvement, meeting and exceeding the highest standards, and always overcoming complacency with the status quo.

Engage Holistically

Olympic athletes know what it means to invest completely in becoming the best they can be, but by narrowly focusing on their sport they often truncate their full development. Swimmer Michael Phelps's mantra prior to the Beijing Olympics was "eat, sleep, and swim." For the years leading up to the Olympics his monastic life extended only to a small apartment, an iPod, a swimming pool, and a handful of restaurants where he could quickly consume enough calories to support his rigorous swimming schedule.

To become fully human requires that same kind of devotion but scattered across every area of your life. Just as your body needs a balanced diet, your fullest development requires nurturing every aspect of your life without allowing any one of them to diminish the others. Finding your passion is important, but so is sustaining your passion for each aspect of your life. God wants us to be well and to be well is to be whole. Discovering the balance of mind, spirit, creativity, work, and relationship requires attentiveness to your soul and a willingness to be corrected by God, by circumstances, and by the people in your life.

Go Deep

Within you is a fathomless reservoir of possibilities and your soul's capacity is deeper than any ocean. As the old saying goes, boats are safe in the harbor, but that's not what boats are for. You will never become who you are destined to be unless you push out of the shallows and into the depths of who you might become. For centuries ancient cultures passed the lessons of previous generations from one to the next so the repertoire of responses of the current generation could be rooted firmly in the lessons of the past. Realms of the spirit, insights into the nature of existence, embedded intuitions about the universe itself—all these are deep within our collective consciousness and in the wise writings of diverse cultures both ancient and contemporary. Still waters run deep, and the settled spirit of the full human is the product of becoming a person of substance. As Angelus Silesius said, "Come drink and have your fill, all is for you and free; Divinity itself shall your banquet be."[3]

Grow Each Day in Each Way

A ravenously curious intellect, a warm loving spirit, an imaginative playfulness, a quest for purity, a deep reservoir of love, and a taproot sunk deep into God—these are the keys to renewing yourself completely each day, again and again. Jazz impresario Miles Davis once said, "Don't play what you know; play what you don't know." To grow means to move beyond where you are, for if you are not growing you are dying. Just as a plant needs sunshine, rain, good soil, and a lot of time, learn what nurtures your total person and make sure those elements are in place in your daily life. Include rest in the list, for the best wine is grown where the vineyards are allowed to lie fallow and replenish.

Don't Give Up

Every day some give up on their quest to become the best they can be. Don't ever give up. You will certainly experience setbacks, discouraging words, disillusioning experiences, and intermittent harsh blasts of cold air on your tender warm spirit. Perhaps a personal weakness will be exposed that you had previously seen only as a strength. Maybe you are simply weary of seeking to advance and after years of struggle, it seems not to be worth it anymore. When Fred Astaire went to his first screen test a written report came back saying, "Can't act. Can't sing. Can dance a little." He persevered, and proved them wrong!

Battle fatigue is common in war, and seeking to become fully human in a fallen world demands persistence and stamina. Those who succeed have learned what the Celtic Book of Prayer reminds us, "Seasons of joy, seasons of sorrow, times when the Lord is so real it seems any activity you undertake is a spiritual experience. Seasons of dryness, when things are so bleak that even a plateful of Sinai sand would be considered a feast! Are not these seasons from the hand of God? If so, what is His goal in the matter? He is taking you to a place where you can be a man for all seasons."[4] Cherish and do not waste what God is doing in your life.

Serve

Those who are fully alive have learned that it is in dying to ourselves and in serving others that we find the eternal and abundant life of God's kingdom. Make it your aim to make a life, not just a living, and make serving others your daily practice. Anticipate the needs of those around you and attend to them without being asked. The late actor Paul Newman was known for his line of products whose proceeds go to charity. Not long before he died he confessed, "We are such spendthrifts with our lives. The trick of living is to slip on and off the planet with the least fuss you can muster. I'm not running for sainthood. I just happen to think that in life we need to be a little like the farmer, who puts back into the soil what he takes out."[5] Be the happiness maker whose needs are kept simple and whose capacity to give and love is ever expanding.

Collaborate

Who are the people you are partnering with? What talents do you bring? What talents might others bring that will complement and complete yours? There is a magic and power in teamwork, as Mr. Rogers once illustrated in a touching story of something that happened at the Special Olympics. Nine contestants, all of them so-called physically or mentally disabled, were competing in the hundred-yard dash. All nine assembled at the starting line and at the sound of the gun, took off. But not long afterward one little boy stumbled and fell and hurt his knee and began to cry. The other eight children heard him crying; they slowed down, turned around, and ran back to him. Every one of them ran back to him. One little girl with Down's syndrome bent down and kissed the boy and said, "This'll make it better." And the little boy got up and he and the rest of the runners linked their arms together and joyfully walked to the finish line. They all finished the race at the same time. And when they did, everyone in that stadium stood up and clapped and whistled and cheered for a long, long time. People who were there are still telling the story with great delight. And you know why. Because deep down, we know that what matters in this life is more than winning for ourselves. What really matters is helping others win too, even if it means slowing down and changing our course now and then.[6]

Recognize This as a Fallen World That Needs Healing and Salvation

To become fully human is to remain clear in our knowledge that our civilization is dying spiritually, morally, creatively, intellectually, and in a myriad of other ways. We cannot be comfortable with the status quo of this fallen world. Jesus repeatedly said that personal and cultural transformation starts with a new heart, a conclusion reached by Vaclav Havel, the Czech playwright, essayist, and former dissident and politician. He said, "The salvation of the human world lies nowhere else but in the human heart, in the human power to reflect, in human modesty, and in personal responsibility. Without a global reevaluation in this sphere of human consciousness, nothing will change for the better . . . and the catastrophe toward which this world is headed, whether it be ecological, social, demographic, or a general breakdown of civilization, will be unavoidable."[7] With eyes to see, new hearts and clear minds, we must take our gifts and invest them in this needy world. This world may not be our ultimate home, and we may just be passing through, but we will spend each day as a loving, transforming presence, just as Jesus did.

Aim for Heaven

After British journalist Malcolm Muggeridge returned to the Christian faith he realized his whole life had been consumed with a longing for the eternal: "The first thing I remember about the world—and I pray it may be the last—is that I was a stranger in it. This feeling, which everyone has in some degree, and which is at once the glory and desolation of homo sapiens, provides the only thread of consistency that I can see in my life."[8] Having left the garden we can never return to its innocence, but having glimpsed the eternal in this life, we desire to taste more of the eternal now. This is why C. S. Lewis advised Christians: "Aim at heaven and you will get earth thrown in. Aim at earth and you get neither." Our quest for a fully alive, fully human life begins now; its ultimate fulfillment comes when this life ends and our new life begins, when we are fully reunited with our creator in eternity.

Finally, I was raised to believe that the way to please God was to receive Jesus, live a good life, and tell others about Jesus. This was not bad advice, just incomplete. St. Irenaeus stated a more complete aim when he said, "The glory of God is man fully alive."

I have observed that some people lose their way spiritually and others lose their way humanly. Some believe to be spiritual means to suppress their humanness, and others believe to live a full human life requires rejecting the spiritual. Our journey toward being fully alive and fully human requires seeing Jesus' incarnation as a model for our own wholeness. He was fully God and fully human, and only the fullest integration of our humanness and spirituality will produce the well person we wish to be.

Remember: The Best Is Yet to Come

There was an off-Broadway play titled I *Love You, You're Perfect, Now Change*. That title captures my final piece of advice. I love you, you're perfect, now change. The more God becomes central in this life, the more you are prepared to join God in the next life. The more you aim for fullness in this life, the more you realize you hunger for things in another world. We will enter that other world through our death or when Jesus returns, whichever comes first. We began in a garden with a tree that led to our unraveling. Jesus went to the cross, a tree on which he died, so that our restoration as a new kind of human could begin. Now we lean forward in hopes of yet another tree, the tree of life that is found in heaven next to the river of life and described by John, whose vision is recorded in the apocalyptic Book of Revelation.

> Then the angel showed me the river of the water of
> life, as clear as crystal, flowing from the throne of
> God and of the Lamb down the middle of the great
> street of the city. On each side of the river stood the
> tree of life, bearing twelve crops of fruit, yielding
> its fruit every month. And the leaves of the tree are

for the healing of the nations. No longer will there
be any curse. The throne of God and of the Lamb
will be in the city, and his servants will serve him.
They will see his face, and his name will be on their
foreheads. There will be no more night. They will
not need the light of a lamp or the light of the sun,
for the Lord God will give them light. And they will
reign forever and ever (Revelation 22:1–22).

C. S. Lewis describes our future hope dramatically at
the conclusion of the Narnia series when he says, "For us
this is the end of all the stories. But for them it was only the
beginning of the real story. All their life in this world had
only been the cover and the title page: now at last they were
beginning Chapter One of the Great Story, which no one on
earth has read, which goes on forever and in which every
chapter is better than the one before."[9]

Our destiny is with God, where the nations are healed
by leaves from the tree of life and where we drink life-
giving water. There the radiance of God is all the light we
need and in that place is found no heartache, no tears, no
sorrow. For us the end is the wonderful beginning of the
real story, for in heaven, the poem God has been writing of
our earthly life will find its completion and we will be fully
alive and fully human forever.

afterword: a creed for the fully human

I am a masterpiece, a genius, who, to be satisfied in this life and the next, simply must reach my fullest potential. The glory of God is a human fully alive, and to go to the grave with my song still in me would dishonor my creator and diminish me.

I am of great worth. Because I bear a unique imprint of God's image, I possess distinct spiritual, intellectual, creative, and relational capacities ready to be developed and expressed. What I share with other humans is greater than our differences, and I will treat others with the respect appropriate for their role as God's image bearers.

I've been created for union with God and companionship and collaboration with others. Becoming fully human and living a rich fulfilling life is something I accomplish together with others, not alone.

I understand how humans got off-track, what sickness it is that diminished and dehumanized us, and why it is that we feel broken and incomplete. I know why I long for circumstances more suitable for my fullest development, why I intuitively sense something is wrong with this world.

I've come to my senses, I have returned to my creator, I am spiritually alive, I am in the process of being restored to a fully human life, I have identified my unique God-given design. I am developing and expressing God's image imprinted on me in my daily life and work.

I am working for my complete actualization in this life, knowing that Jesus came to make me fully human. But while relishing each day on earth; I am most eager to be reunited with the God I love in another world for which I was made. Then and there, I will be fully and perfectly actualized.

I awaken each day with a sense of hope, energized by what the day may hold, because I know who holds the day and I know I hold within me the potential to live life to the fullest.

notes

Chapter Two: Created

1. *Charles Darwin's Notebook, 1836–1844* (Cambridge: Cambridge University Press, 2009).

2. Francis Crick, *The Astonishing Hypothesis: The Scientific Search for the Soul* (New York: Scribner, 1995), p. 3.

3. Nicholas Wade, "Animals Genetic Program Decoded, in a Science First," *New York Times*, Dec. 11, 1998.

4. Daniel C. Dennett, *Darwin's Dangerous Idea* (New York: Touchstone, 1995), p. 63.

5. Chuck Palahniuk, *Fight Club* (New York: W. W. Norton, 2005), p. 126.

6. *The Dick Staub Show*, Jan. 20, 1994.

7. "Religion of Hatred: Why We Should No Longer Be Cowed by the Chattering Classes Ruling Britain Who Sneer at Christianity." *Daily Mail* (U.K.), Apr. 11, 2009.

8. Mark Eastman, *Creation by Design* (Costa Mesa, CA: T.W.F.T. Publishers, 1996), pp. 21–22.

9. Barbara Bradley Hagerty, *Fingerprints of God: The Search for the Science of Spirituality* (New York: Riverhead Hardcover, 2009).

10. Robert Sokolowski, *Christian Faith & Human Understanding: Studies on the Eucharist, the Trinity, and the Human Person* (Washington, DC: Catholic University of America Press, 2006), p. 161.

Chapter Three: In God's Image

1. Nevada Barr, *Seeking Enlightenment, Hat by Hat: A Skeptic's Guide to Religion* (Berkeley: University of California Press, 2004), p. 3.

2. Dorothy Sayers, *The Mind of the Maker* (San Francisco: HarperOne, 1987).

Chapter Four: Together

1. Howard Baetzhold and Joseph McCullough, eds., *The Bible According to Mark Twain* (New York: Simon & Schuster, 1995), pp. 3–34.

2. David Carr, "Woody Harrelson Loves the Beach, the Planet and Movies," *New York Times*, Nov. 25, 2007.

3. C. S. Lewis, *The Weight of Glory* (New York: HarperCollins, 2001), p. 157.

4. Baetzhold and McCullough, p. 31.

Chapter Five: Our Ancestral Homeland

1. Frederick Buechner, *The Longing for Home* (New York: HarperCollins, 1996), p. 18.

2. A. W. Tozer, *Tozer on the Almighty God: A 366-day Devotional* (Camp Hill, PA: WingSpread Publishers, 2007).

3. Somerset Maugham, *The Moon and Sixpence* (Mineoloa, NY: Dover Publications, 2006), p. 101.

Chapter Six: Fallen, Broken, and Sick unto Death

1. Mel Gussow, "For Saul Bellow, Seeing the Earth with Fresh Eyes" [interview with Saul Bellow], *New York Times*, May 26, 1997.

2. George Carlin, *Complaints and Grievances, People Who Oughta Be Killed* (Atlanta: Self-Help Books, 2001).

3. Edward E. Ericson Jr., "Solzhenitsyn—Voice from the Gulag," *Eternity Magazine*, 1985, pp. 23, 24.

4. Dag Hammarskjold, *Markings* (New York: Vintage Books, 2006), p. 46.

Chapter Seven: Alone in a Hostile Land

1. C. S. Lewis, *Mere Christianity* (San Francisco: HarperOne, 2001), p. 46.

2. C. S. Lewis, *The Great Divorce* (New York: HarperCollins, 2009), p. 65.

3. T. S. Eliot, *Christianity and Culture* (New York: Harcourt Brace Jovanovitch, 1967).

4. Harry Blamires, *The Christian Mind* (Vancouver: Regent College Publishing, 2005).

5. Editorial, *Wall Street Journal*, Dec. 12, 1991.

Chapter Eight: Coming to Your Senses

1. Douglas Coupland, *Life After God* (New York: Washington Square Press, 1995), p. 359.

2. *National Review*, Feb. 24, 1997, p. 55.

3. *The Dick Staub Show*, interview with Robert Stone, May 5, 1998.

4. Malcolm Muggeridge, *A Spiritual Evolution* [Muggeridge's conversion experience summarized]. http://www.thewords.com/articles/mugquest.htm.

5. Herman Melville, *Moby Dick* (New York: Oxford University Press, 2008), p. 73.

Chapter Nine: Returning

1. Blaise Pascal, *Pensées* (New York: Penguin, 1995), p. 52.

2. Meg Ryan, *Readers Digest*, Feb. 1, 2002.

3. Robert Bellah, Richard Madsen, William M. Sullivan, Ann Swidler, and Steven M. Tipton, *Habits of the Heart* (Berkeley: University of California Press, 2007), p. 221.

4. C. S. Lewis, *Surprised by Joy* (New York: Houghton Mifflin Harcourt, 1995), p. 220.

5. *The Dick Staub Show*, interview with Rick Moody, Sept. 1, 2002.

Chapter Ten: Awaking from the Dead

1. Rebecca Johnson, "Notes on a Scandal," *Vogue*, Aug. 2009.

2. John Heilemann and Mark Halperin, "Game Change: Obama and the Clintons, McCain and Palin, and the Race of a Lifetime," *Harper Magazine*, Jan. 11, 2010.

3. Read the entire story in the Old Testament Book of Ezekiel, ch. 37.

4. Read this story in the Gospel of John, ch. 11.

5.**1. Hearing.** Matthew 13:15: For this people's heart has become calloused; they hardly hear with their ears, and they have closed their eyes. Otherwise they might see with their eyes, hear with their ears, understand with their hearts and turn, and I would heal them. Matthew 13:16: But blessed are your eyes because they see, and your ears because they hear. Mark 4:9: Then Jesus said, "He who has ears to hear, let him hear." Luke 11:28: He replied, "Blessed rather are those who hear the word of God and obey it."

2. Believing. John 20:31: But these are written that you may believe that Jesus is the Christ, the Son of God, and that by believing you may have life in his name. Mark 1:15: "The time has come," he said. "The kingdom of God is near. Repent and believe the good news!" Mark 16:16: Whoever believes and is baptized will be saved, but whoever does not believe will be condemned. John 1:12: Yet to all who received him, to those who believed in his name, he gave the right to become children of God. John 3:18: Whoever believes in him is not condemned, but whoever does not believe stands condemned already because he has not believed in the name of God's one and only Son. John 11:26: And whoever lives and believes in me will never die. John 11:27: "Yes, Lord," she told him, "I believe that you are the Christ, the Son of God, who was to come into the world." Acts 16:31: They replied, "Believe in the Lord Jesus, and you will be saved—you and your household." Romans 10:9–11: That if you confess with your mouth, "Jesus is Lord," and believe in your heart that God raised him from the dead, you will be saved. For it is with your heart that you believe and are justified, and it is with your mouth that you confess and are saved. As the Scripture says, "Anyone who trusts in him will never be put to shame."

3. Confessing. Romans 10:9–11: That if you confess with your mouth, "Jesus is Lord," and believe in your heart that God raised him from the dead, you will be saved. For it is with your heart that you believe and are justified, and it is with your mouth that you confess and are saved. As the Scripture says, "Anyone who trusts in him will never be put to shame." 1 John 1:9: If we confess our sins, he is faithful and just and will forgive us our sins and purify us from all unrighteousness.

4. **Repenting.** Matthew 4:7: From that time on Jesus began to preach, "Repent, for the kingdom of heaven is near." Mark 1:15: "The time has come," he said. "The kingdom of God is near. Repent and believe the good news!" Mark 6:12: They went out and preached that people should repent. Acts 2:38: Peter replied, "Repent and be baptized, every one of you, in the name of Jesus Christ for the forgiveness of your sins. And you will receive the gift of the Holy Spirit." Acts 3:9: Repent, then, and turn to God, so that your sins may be wiped out, that times of refreshing may come from the Lord. Acts 26:20: First to those in Damascus, then to those in Jerusalem and in all Judea, and to the Gentiles also, I preached that they should repent and turn to God and prove their repentance by their deeds.

5. **Denying yourself, taking up a cross, following Jesus.** Matthew 16:24, Mark 8:34: Then Jesus said to his disciples, "If anyone would come after me, he must deny himself and take up his cross and follow me." Luke 9:23: Then he said to them all: "If anyone would come after me, he must deny himself and take up his cross daily and follow me."

6. **Receiving.** John 1:12: Yet to all who received him, to those who believed in his name, he gave the right to become children of God. Mark 10:15: I tell you the truth, anyone who will not receive the kingdom of God like a little child will never enter it. Acts 1:8: But you will receive power when the Holy Spirit comes on you; and you will be my witnesses in Jerusalem, and in all Judea and Samaria, and to the ends of the earth.

7. **Loving.** Matthew 5:44: But I tell you: Love your enemies and pray for those who persecute you. Matthew 19:19: Honor your father and mother, and love your neighbor as

yourself. Matthew 22:36–40: Teacher, which is the greatest
commandment in the Law? 37: Jesus replied: "'Love the
Lord your God with all your heart and with all your soul
and with all your mind.' 38: This is the first and greatest
commandment. 39: And the second is like it: 'Love your
neighbor as yourself.' 40: All the Law and the Prophets hang
on these two commandments." John 13:34–35: A new
command I give you: Love one another. As I have loved you,
so you must love one another. By this all men will know that
you are my disciples, if you love one another. John 14:21:
Whoever has my commands and obeys them, he is the one
who loves me. He who loves me will be loved by my Father,
and I too will love him and show myself to him.

8. **Growing.** Luke 8: 5–15: "A farmer went out to sow his seed.
As he was scattering the seed, some fell along the path; it was
trampled on, and the birds of the air ate it up. 6: Some fell
on rock, and when it came up, the plants withered because
they had no moisture. 7: Other seed fell among thorns, which
grew up with it and choked the plants. 8: Still other seed fell
on good soil. It came up and yielded a crop, a hundred times
more than was sown." When he said this, he called out, "He
who has ears to hear, let him hear." 9: His disciples asked him
what this parable meant. 10: He said, "The knowledge of the
secrets of the kingdom of God has been given to you, but to
others I speak in parables, so that, 'though seeing, they may
not see; though hearing, they may not understand.'" 11: This
is the meaning of the parable: The seed is the word of God.
12: Those along the path are the ones who hear, and then the
devil comes and takes away the word from their hearts, so that
they may not believe and be saved. 13: Those on the rock are
the ones who receive the word with joy when they hear it,
but they have no root. They believe for a while, but in the time
of testing they fall away. 14: The seed that fell among thorns
stands for those who hear, but as they go on their way they
are choked by life's worries, riches, and pleasures, and they
do not mature. 15: But the seed on good soil stands for those

with a noble and good heart, who hear the word, retain it, and by persevering produce a crop. Galatians 5:22: The fruit of the Spirit is love, joy, peace, patience, kindness, goodness, faithfulness. 23: Gentleness and self-control.

9. **Obeying.** John 14:21: Whoever has my commands and obeys them, he is the one who loves me. He who loves me will be loved by my Father, and I too will love him and show myself to him. Matthew 28:18: Then Jesus came to them and said, "All authority in heaven and on earth has been given to me. 19: Therefore go and make disciples of all nations, baptizing them in the name of the Father and of the Son and of the Holy Spirit. 20: And teaching them to obey everything I have commanded you. And surely I am with you always, to the very end of the age." Luke 11:28: He replied, "Blessed rather are those who hear the word of God and obey it." Acts 5:32: We are witnesses of these things, and so is the Holy Spirit, whom God has given to those who obey him.

Chapter Eleven: The Humanizing Jesus

1. Frederick Franck, *What Matters: Spiritual Nourishment for Head and Heart* (Skylight Paths Publishing, 2004).

2. Eugene Peterson, *The Contemplative Pastor: Returning to the Art of Spiritual Direction* (Grand Rapids, MI: Wm. B. Erdmans, 1993), p. 54.

3. St. Athanasius, *On the Incarnation* (Create Space, Oct. 4, 2007), p. 14.

4. C. S. Lewis, *Screwtape Letters* (New York: HarperCollins, 2001), p. 72.

5. **We die because of Adam; we have new life because of Jesus.** For as in Adam all die, so in Christ all will be made alive (1 Corinthians 15:22).

Our human lineage is in Adam; our spiritual lineage begins with Jesus, the last Adam.

The first man Adam became a living being; the last Adam, a life-giving spirit (1 Corinthians 15:45).

Jesus' resurrection makes him the firstborn from the dead and the beginning of a new race of humans. Jesus Christ is the faithful witness, the firstborn from the dead, and the ruler of the kings of the earth. To him who loves us and has freed us from our sins by his blood, and has made us to be a kingdom and priests to serve his God and Father—to him be glory and power forever and ever! Amen (Revelation 1:5, 6).

The firstborn of a new creation perfectly reflects the image of God. Jesus is the image of the invisible God, the firstborn over all creation. For by him all things were created: things in heaven and on earth, visible and invisible, whether thrones or powers or rulers or authorities; all things were created by him and for him. He is before all things, and in him all things hold together. He is the beginning and the firstborn from among the dead, so that in everything he might have the supremacy (Colossians 1:15–17).

Jesus is the fullness of God and because of him we are fully reconciled to God and are no longer alienated from God. For God was pleased to have all his fullness dwell in him, and through him to reconcile to himself all things, whether things on earth or things in heaven, by making peace through his blood, shed on the cross. Once you were alienated from God and were enemies in your minds because of your evil behavior (Colossians 1:22). But now he has reconciled you by Christ's physical body through death to present you holy in his sight, without blemish and free from accusation (Colossians 1:18–22).

Jesus came to begin a new race of humans. While this truth is woven throughout the whole Bible, the apostle Paul puts it most succinctly when he says, "If anyone is in Christ, he or she is a new creature; old things are passed away, all things become new (2 Corinthians 5:17).

Chapter Twelve: Restoring

1.   Howard Gardner, *Multiple Intelligences: New Horizons in Theory and Practice* (New York: Basic Books, 2006).

2. Paul Clasper, "C. S. Lewis's Contribution to a 'Missionary Theology': An Asian Perspective," *CSL The Bulletin of the New York C. S. Lewis Society* 12:9 (July 1981), 6.

Chapter Thirteen

1. I recommend *Finding a Job You Can Love*, by Arthur F. Miller Jr. and Ralph Mattson (P & R Publishing, 1999); *Passion and Purpose: How to Identify and Leverage the Powerful Patterns That Shape Your Work/Life*, by Merle E. Hanson and Arthur F. Miller Jr. (Marlys Hanson & Associates, 2002). For professional assistance I refer you to Art Miller III at artpmi@gmail .com and Don Kiehl at dkiehl@simainternational.com.

2. Dick Staub's Motivated Abilities Pattern (Intercristo, Mar. 18, 1982, Updated May 1990 PMGI copyright © People Management).

CENTRAL THRUST (*primary result you want to achieve*)
IMPRESS—IMPACT ON—MAKE MARK, SHAPE
BUILD—DEVELOP—FORM
EXTRACT—ACHIEVE POTENTIAL

MOTIVATED ABILITIES

LEARNING	By studying, reading
EVALUATING	By comparing to standard, appraising, assessing
CONCEPTUALIZING	By formulating concepts, developing precepts
ORGANIZING	By structuring, providing definition
PLANNING	By setting goals, by strategizing charting a course
CREATING	By conceiving
DEVELOPING	By growing, cultivating; building up by adapting, modifying, improvising
OVERSEEING	By directing how it is to be done

| INFLUENCING | By selling, confronting, by motivating, inspiring by involving, getting participation |
| COMMUNICATING | By articulating, explaining/by public speaking, giving presentations |

SUBJECT MATTER

IDEAS	MONEY FINANCIAL MATTERS
CONCEPTS	PEOPLE-GENERAL
KNOWLEDGE,	PEOPLE-INDIVIDUALS
INFORMATION	CONTROLS, CONSTRAINTS
THOUGHTS, EXPRESSION	
STRATEGIES, TACTICS,	
ANGLES	

MOTIVATING CIRCUMSTANCES

APPLICATION INVOLVED	GROUP, TEAM
NEW, NOVEL, DIFFERENT	GROWTH, DEVELOPING
(to achiever)	PROJECT, PROGRAM
DIFFICULTIES, OBSTACLES	PROFITABILITY
GOAL, OBJECTIVE	POTENTIAL, POSSIBLE
TESTS CHALLENGES	EFFECTIVENESS (rather than known, sure)
SUGGESTED FUNCTION	ENTREPRENEURIAL

OPERATING RELATIONSHIP WITH OTHERS

DIRECTIVE SPEARHEAD
INDIVIDUALIST
(in team context)

3. C. S. Lewis, *The Weight of Glory* (San Francisco: HarperOne, 2001), p. 46.

Chapter Fourteen : And in the End, a Beginning

1. C. S Lewis, *Mere Christianity* (San Francisco: HarperOne, 2001), pp. 136–137.

2. Corinne Roosevelt Robinson, *The Poems of Corinne Roosevelt Robinson* (BiblioLife, 2008), p. 17.

3. Angelus Silesius, *The Cherubinic Wanderer* (Mahwah, NJ: Paulist Press, 1986).

4. *Celtic Daily Prayer: Prayers and Readings from the Northumbria Community* (New York: HarperCollins, 2002).

5. Paul Newman Obituary, *New York Times*, Sept. 27, 2008, New York ed., p. 1.

6. Fred Rogers, commencement address, Dartmouth College, June 9, 2002.

7. Vaclev Havel, address to the U.S. Congress, Feb. 1990.

8. Ian Hunter, *Malcolm Muggeridge: A Life* (Vancouver: Regent College Publishing, 2003), p. 12.

9. C. S. Lewis, *Chronicles of Narnia* (New York: HarperCollins, Collectors ed., 2006).